ELEMENTS

OF

LOGICK;

OR A

SUMMARY OF THE GENERAL PRINCIPLES
AND DIFFERENT MODES

OF

REASONING.

BY

LEVI HEDGE, LL. D.,

PROFESSOR OF NATURAL RELIGION, MORAL PHILOSOPHY, AND
CIVIL POLITY, IN HARVARD UNIVERSITY.

WIPF & STOCK · Eugene, Oregon

Wipf and Stock Publishers
199 W 8th Ave, Suite 3
Eugene, OR 97401

Elements of Logick
Or a Summary of the General Principles and
Different Modes of Reasoning
By Hedge, Levi
ISBN 13: 978-1-60608-497-7
Publication date 6/4/2009
Previously published by Phinney, Blakeman, & Mason, 1861

PREFACE

TO THE FIRST EDITION.

Most of the treatises of Logick in common use have been formed on the model of the ancient systems, and are encumbered with many scholastick subtilties and unimportant distinctions. The instructions, which they furnish on the subject of ratiocination, consist of very little more than a description of the syllogism, and a few general principles of demonstrative reasoning. They contain no elements nor rules to assist us in reasoning on subjects of probability, or on the ordinary events of human life. The manner, in which these books are written, is ill adapted to the comprehension of young minds. In explaining the operations of reasoning, many technical terms and arbitrary forms are employed, of which the tendency is rather to embarrass and perplex, than to instruct the learner.

Though much has been written, of late years, on the powers and operations of the mind, yet there have been but few attempts to form a system of Logick for the use of those, who are commencing the study. Collard has improved the syllogism, by simplifying its principles, and divesting it of its ancient trappings of modes and figures. Condillac has proved the importance of the method of induction, by pointing out the manner, in which Nature teaches us to analyze the objects, which she presents to our observation. In "An Essay on the Elements, Principles, and different Modes of Reasoning," by Richard Kirwan, LL. D., all the subjects, which properly fall within the precincts of Logick, are amply discussed. But this work is too minute and prolix to be used as a text book in seminaries of education. Every person who is much conversant with this department of knowledge, must have perceived the want of a treatise of Logick, more elementary, and better accommodated to the present improved state of the philosophy of the mind, than any of those, which are now in use.

The professed object of Logick is to furnish rules for the direction of the understanding in its various inquiries after knowledge. It should, therefore, teach the principles of every species of reasoning, which we have occasion to make use of, both in the pursuits of science, and in the ordinary transactions of life. Demonstrative reasoning can be employed only about general truths, and such relations as are in their nature immutable. It is of little use in regulating our judgments and conclusions concerning events, which are irregular in their occurrence, and which depend on contingent circumstances. To reason on subjects of this kind, it is necessary to understand the nature of moral evidence, and the grounds of probability. It is by moral evidence alone, that we reason on historical facts, and the casual occurrences of life. It is also this evidence, which influences our conclusions on the important and interesting subjects of government, morals, and religion.

Under these impressions, the writer of this compend has pursued the following plan. After passing through the customary distinctions of terms and propositions, he has given a brief account of moral evidence, and pointed out the circumstances, which distinguish it from demonstrative. A concise view is then given of the different forms of reasoning, with the principles, on which they respectively proceed.

The books, which have been principally consulted in forming this summary, and in which the greatest part of the following principles may be found, are Watts's Logick, Locke's Essay on the Understanding, Reid's Essays on the Intellectual Powers, Stewart's Elements of the Philosophy of the Mind, Beattie's Essay on Truth, Tatham's Chart and Scale of Truth, Collard's Essentials of Logick, Kirwan's Logick, Campbell's Philosophy of Rhetorick, Gambier's Introduction to Moral Evidence, Belsham's Compendium of Logick, and Scott's Elements of Intellectual Philosophy.

Where passages have been borrowed entire, credit is given in the usual way. At the close of the several chapters may be found the names of those authors, from whom particular assistance has been derived.

PREFACE

TO THE THIRD EDITION.

THE present edition of the elements of Logick is printed in a smaller type than either of the preceding, in order that the copies may be afforded at a reduced price. The author has carefully revised the work, and has enlarged it by the addition of a few pages, containing some general principles and rules respecting controversy, and also a system of rules for the interpretation of written documents. These have been collected with care from authors of high reputation, and, it is hoped, will not be thought an unsuitable appendage to a system of logick. In a few places, slight alterations have been made in the language and in the arrangement; and some notes have been inserted at the end of the book, which were not in the preceding editions.

Harvard College, Nov. 1821.

ADVERTISEMENT TO EDITION OF 1849.

This edition is printed on entirely new plates. As the work in its present form appears to have been generally approved in the colleges and higher schools in which it has so long been a text-book, no alterations have been made from the previous editions.

CONTENTS.

PART FIRST.

A DESCRIPTION OF THE LEADING AFFECTIONS AND OPERATIONS OF THE MIND.

	Page
INTRODUCTION.	13

CHAPTER I.
Perception and Consciousness. 14

CHAPTER II.
Attention. 19

CHAPTER III.
Comparing. 21

CHAPTER IV.
Abstraction. 23

CHAPTER V.
Association. 25

CHAPTER VI.
Analysis. 28

PART SECOND.

OF TERMS AND PROPOSITIONS.

CHAPTER I.
Logical Distinctions of Terms. . . . 31

CONTENTS.

CHAPTER II.
Definition and Division. 39

CHAPTER III.
General Description of Propositions. . . . 43

CHAPTER IV.
Simple, Complex, and Modal Propositions. . . 47

CHAPTER V
Quality and Quantity of Propositions. . . . 50

CHAPTER VI.
Opposition and Conversion of Propositions. . . 55

CHAPTER VII.
Compound Propositions. 59

PART THIRD.

OF JUDGMENT AND REASONING.

CHAPTER I.
Intuitive Evidence. 65

CHAPTER II.
Difference between Moral and Demonstrative Reasoning. 70

CHAPTER III.
Induction. 76

CHAPTER IV.
Analogy. 83

CHAPTER V.
Reasoning on Facts. 88

CHAPTER VI.
Calculation of Chances. 101

CHAPTER VII.
General Description of Demonstrative Reasoning. 108

CHAPTER VIII.
Distinctions of Reasoning. 113

CHAPTER IX.
General Description of Syllogistick Reasoning. . 116

CHAPTER X.
Regular Syllogisms. 120

CHAPTER XI.
Enthymemes. 130

CHAPTER XII.
Conditional and Disjunctive Syllogisms. . . . 134

CHAPTER XIII.
Compound Syllogisms. 137

CHAPTER XIV.
Sophisms. 144

CHAPTER XV.
Disposition or Method. 149

CHAPTER XVI.
Rules of Controversy. 157

CHAPTER XVII.
Rules of Interpretation. 162
CONCLUDING REMARKS. 168
NOTES AND ILLUSTRATIONS. . . . 171

ELEMENTS OF LOGICK.

PART FIRST.

DESCRIPTION OF THE LEADING AFFECTIONS AND OPERATIONS OF THE MIND.

INTRODUCTION.

1. *The purpose of Logick is to direct the intellectual powers in the investigation of truth, and in the communication of it to others.* Its foundation is laid in the philosophy of the human mind, inasmuch as it explains many of its powers and operations, and traces the progress of knowledge, from the first and most simple perceptions of outward objects, to those remoter truths and discoveries, which result from the operations of reasoning.

2. Logick instructs us in the right use of terms, and distinguishes their various kinds. It teaches the nature and varieties of propositions; explains their properties, modifications,

and essential parts. It analyzes the structure of arguments, and shows how their truth may be discovered, or their fallacy detected. Lastly, it describes those *methods* of classification and arrangement, which will best enable us to retain and apply the knowledge, which we have acquired.

3. Though the understanding would be incapable of any high degree of improvement, without the aid of rules and principles, yet these are insufficient without practice and experience. The powers of the mind, like those of the body, must be strengthened by use. The art of reasoning skilfully can be acquired only by a long and careful exercise of the reasoning faculty, on different subjects and in various ways. The rules of logick afford assistance to this faculty, not less important than that, which our animal strength derives from the aid of mechanical powers and engines. They guide its operations, and supply it with suitable instruments for overcoming the difficulties, by which it would be impeded in its search after truth.

4. In the following compend, the subjects of logick are distributed into three parts. The

first contains a brief description of the leading powers and operations of the mind: The second, of the several kinds of terms and propositions. The third comprises an explanation of moral and demonstrative evidence; of the different modes of reasoning; of sophisms; and of method, or disposition.

CHAPTER FIRST.
PERCEPTION AND CONSCIOUSNESS.

5. *Perception* is the first state or affection of the human mind. By this we gain all our knowledge of the powers and qualities of the material objects about us. The instruments of perception are the five corporeal senses, seeing, feeling, hearing, tasting, and smelling. All the intercourse, which the mind has with the material world, is carried on by these organs. Of the manner, in which this intercourse proceeds, we have no knowledge. From experience we learn, that a sensible alteration takes place in the mind, whenever any outward object is so situated, as to affect either of the senses. The *change*, produced in the mind by the impression of the object on the organ of sense, is denominated *sensation*.

The word *perception denotes the knowledge, that we gain by sensation, of some quality in the object;** which knowledge may be retained by the mind after the object is removed, and it is then usually called an *idea* or *notion*. The external object, or quality perceived, is denominated the *object* of *perception*, or the *archetype* of the idea.

6. If either of the senses be wholly wanting, the mind must be forever destitute of all that class of ideas, which it is the office of that sense to furnish. If either be possessed but imperfectly, the ideas, received from it, are liable to be faint and indistinct. But the usual effects of dull organs may be in a great measure obviated, by an increased effort of attention, while the objects are present; as is manifest in the case of persons, who have had their hearing in some degree impaired.

It is from habitual inattention to our sensations, more than from dulness in the organs

---

* " The *sensations*, which are excited in the mind by external " objects, and the *perceptions* of material qualities, which follow those " sensations, are to be distinguished from each other only by long " habits of patient reflection." *Stewart, Elem.* vol. i. ch. v. part 2d sect 1st.

of sense, that so few of the objects, which strike our senses, leave any durable traces in the mind; and that those notions, which do remain, are so often obscure and indistinct. As the perceptions of sense are the first elements of our knowledge, we should cultivate the habit of carefully noticing the things, which we see, feel, and the like; in order that the notions, which we form of them, may be clear and distinct.

7. *Consciousness, or reflection, is that notice, which the mind takes of its own operations, and modes of existence.** By this we are made acquainted with the successive changes, which take place in the state of our minds. Consciousness is similar to perception, though the qualities of body, which are the objects of the latter, bear no resemblance to the thoughts and operations of the mind, which are the objects of the former. The mind, at least whilst we are awake, is constantly employed in some mode of thinking, or in some exertion of its powers; and all the operations, passions, and affections of the mind, are necessarily subject to its own observation. Thus, by

* See note A, at the end of the book.

consciousness, we learn what is expressed by the words *compare, reason, doubt, assent, joy* in the same manner as, by perception, we gain a knowledge of *sweet, green, soft, cold.*

8. *Both perception and consciousness, considered apart from any acts of attention, accompanying them, are involuntary states of mind.* We are often active in bringing external objects within our view, and in varying their position, for the purpose of careful observation; so, by a voluntary effort, we excite operations, and cause changes in the mind; but the knowledge, that we gain in each case, of the subjects thus presented, is without any act of the will. We cannot avoid hearing many sounds, and seeing the objects, which are placed before our eyes. We are constrained to smell odours, taste our food, and feel bodies, when in contact with our own. It is the same with respect to the operations and states of the mind. We are unable to compare, reason, abstract; to feel pain, pleasure, disgust, or the like, without being conscious of those states.

CHAPTER SECOND.
ATTENTION.

9. *Attention expresses the immediate direction of the mind to a subject.* The distinctness of our notions, the correctness of our judgments, and the improvement of all our intellectual powers, depend, in a great degree, on the habitual excercise of this act. Its surprising influence, in improving the perceptive powers, is manifest in persons, who have been led, by their peculiar callings, or by necessity, to place uncommon reliance on a particular sense.

Thus sailors, who are accustomed to look at distant objects, acquire the power of seeing and distinguishing things, which, by reason of their distance, are invisible to common eyes.* Musicians become capable of discerning the minutest difference in sounds. Cooks and epicures acquire an uncommon sensibility in tasting and smelling; and blind persons improve the sense of feeling to such a degree, as to make it, in some measure, supply the want of sight. These effects are produced chiefly by an increased and habitual attention, which

* A seafaring life, especially when early commenced, has a tendency to produce some physical change in the organ of vision.

enables those persons to notice impressions, which are so slight and languid, as wholly to escape the observation of others.

10. *Attention is considered*[*] *a voluntary act of the mind*, but it is not at all times equally subject to our command, and in young children is wholly involuntary. Extraordinary occurrences, which awaken curiosity, and things, which interest us in a high degree, by exciting some violent passion or emotion, often draw the attention so strongly, that we are unable for a time to transfer it to any other subject. So intensely are we sometimes engaged, that we lose our account of time, and take no notice of the objects, which strike the senses.

11. Attention is so essential to memory, that, without some degree of it, no thought could ever be recalled; and the reason why we commit things to memory more easily at one time, than another, is, that we command our attention more perfectly. It is equally necessary in every operation of comparing, judging, and reasoning. Dr. Reid has remarked, " that, if "there be any thing that can be called *genius*

---

[*] Stewart, Elements of the Philosophy of the Mind, vol. i. ch. 2 Reid, Essays on the Active Powers, Essay II. ch. 3.

"in matters of mere judgment and reasoning,
"it seems to consist chiefly in being able to
"give that attention to the subject, which keeps
"it steady in the mind, till we can survey it
"accurately on all sides. There is a talent
"of imagination, which bounds from earth to
"heaven, and from heaven to earth, in a mo-
"ment. This may be favourable to wit and
"imagery; but the powers of judging and rea-
"soning depend chiefly on keeping the mind
"to a clear and steady view of the subject."*

CHAPTER THIRD.
COMPARING.

12. When the mind contemplates two things in reference to each other, it performs the operation of *comparing*. Thus, when we say iron is harder than lead, and lead is heavier than iron, we compare these two substances with respect to the degrees, in which they possess the qualities of weight and hardness. From this operation we derive all our notions of relation; as *father, cousin, largeness, small-ness, superiority, subjection*, and the like.

* Essays on the Active Powers, Essay II. ch. 3.

We make comparisons with the greatest ease, and frequently without being conscious of them. It is only by this operation, that we are enabled to recognise the objects, which we have before known, or to give to any quality or object an appropriate name; for the application of the name requires not only the sensation, produced by a present object, but the comparison of that sensation with one formerly felt.*

13. This operation is performed by children in their earliest efforts at speech. It is by successively comparing the sounds, they utter, with those, made by others, that they learn to pronounce the words of their native tongue. That propensity to imitation, which is always conspicuous in the sports of children, is happily calculated to improve this effort of the mind. The same may be asserted of many of those studies, which usually occupy the years of childhood, and particularly of the study of foreign languages. Translations from one language into another require a constant and careful comparison of the corresponding words of different languages; an exercise doubly

* Stewart, Elements, vol. i. ch. 5.

important to children, as it serves to improve their discerning faculties, and at the same time leads them to ascertain the exact import of words. The correctness of every process of judgment and reasoning depends, immediately or ultimately, on the accuracy of our comparisons.

CHAPTER FOURTH.

ABSTRACTION.

14. *Abstraction* literally implies the separating of one thing from another; but, as a mental operation, it denotes only a partial consideration of any thing. It is *the act of considering one or more of the properties or circumstances of an object, apart from the rest.* Thus we may consider the length of a bridge, without regarding its breadth or construction. We may speak of fluidity in water, hardness in marble, or sweetness in sugar, without noticing the other properties of those substances. As the quality, thus mentally separated from those existing with it, may be found in numerous subjects, the name applied to it becomes a general term. So *whiteness* stands for the

color of snow, milk, chalk, paper, and many other things.

15. This power, which the mind has, of separating the qualities combined in the objects, which fall under our observation, and of tracing the same quality in a multitude of objects, is the foundation of all classification, and gives rise to the general words of language. But, notwithstanding the necessity of abstraction in every act of classification, it may be performed on individuals, without referring them to any class. This has occasioned some* to suppose, that the formation of classes required a distinct operation, which they called *generalization*. Dr. Reid says, "we cannot "generalize without some degree of abstrac- "tion, but I apprehend we may abstract without "generalizing. For what hinders me from at- "tending to the whiteness of the paper before "me, without applying that color to any other "object? The whiteness of this individual "object is an abstract conception; but not a "general one, while applied to one individual "only. These two operations, however, are

---

* Reid, Intellectual Powers, Essay V. ch. 3. Collard, Logick, part 1. ch. 2.

"subservient to each other; for the more at-
"tributes we observe and distinguish in any
"one individual, the more agreements we shall
"discover between it and other individuals."

CHAPTER FIFTH.
ASSOCIATION.

16. *By the association of ideas is understood that connexion among the thoughts, affections, and operations of the mind, by which one has a tendency to introduce another.* That one idea is often suggested to the mind by another, and that sensible objects revive past trains of thought, are facts familiar to all. Words recall the objects, to which they have been applied; and the objects as readily suggest their names. A long train of associated thoughts is sometimes introduced by a single circumstance. The view of the spot, where we passed the first years of life, after a long absence, will recall many interesting events of childhood. The first notes of a familiar tune, being sounded, will cause the remaining notes to pass through the mind in regular order.

17. No principal of our nature is productive of more important effects, than this, which

establishes a connexion between our ideas, feelings, and mental operations. It is the source of numerous errors and prejudices. It is the foundation of all our local attachments, and of most of our prepossessions in behalf of the government and other institutions of our country. It is to the principle of association, that we are to attribute our predilections for the modes of dress, pronunciation, and behaviour of those, whom we esteem and respect.

The principles of association have been differently stated. Their number is not settled but the following are among the most obvious

18. First, *resemblance* or *analogy* is an extensive principle of association. We are often reminded of one person, by the countenance, voice, or gestures of another. One natural scene suggests another; and one event or one anecdote frequently brings another to our remembrance, by the similarity we observe between them.

19. Secondly, *opposition* or *contrast* is another principle of association, but of less extensive influence than the preceding. The pains of hunger and thirst suggest the pleasures of eating and drinking. Cold reminds us of

heat; darkness, of light; and parsimony, of prodigality. So, among contending parties, extravagance on one side usually drives the other to the opposite extreme.

20. Thirdly, another, and with the bulk of mankind the most extensive, ground of association, is *contiguity* or *nearness of time and place*. The recollection of an event, in which we were interested, brings to our thoughts many circumstances connected with it; as the place we were in, when it happened, or when we were informed of it; the persons, who were with us; and the peculiar state of our feelings at the time. The objects we meet on a road, that we have formerly travelled, successively remind us of the subjects, about which we were employed, when we passed them before.

21. A fourth principle of association results from the relations of *cause* and *effect*, *premises* and *consequences*. The sight of a surgical instrument, or an engine of torture, excites a strong sense of the pain, it is calculated to occasion; and the sight of a wound reminds us of the instrument, by which it was made. When we see a fellow being in distress, we are solicitous to find out the cause; and

when we have afflictive tidings to communicate we anticipate the grief, which will be excited.

22. As one idea may be associated with several others, each leading to a different series, it is obvious, that the same circumstance may suggest different trains of thought to different persons, and to the same person at different times. The association of ideas is concerned in every act of memory and recollection. No thought, after it has once passed from the mind, could ever be recalled, were it not for the tendency of one idea to introduce another.*

CHAPTER SIXTH.

ANALYSIS.

23. *Analysis* deserves a place among the operations, by which the elements of knowledge are acquired. Without this, our perceptive powers would give us only confused and imperfect notions of the objects around us. *To analyze is nothing more, than to distinguish successively the several parts of any compound subject.* Nature dictates this process. We

---

* Hume, Essays, vol. ii. sect. 3. Stewart, Elem. vol. i. ch. 5. Beattie, Dissertations, Mor. and Crit. vol. i. ch. 2, sect. i. Scott Elem. Intel. Phil. ch. v. sect. i.

commence it at the earliest period of improvement, and practise it in all our efforts to obtain information. The objects, which nature presents to us, consist of assemblages of different qualities, some more and others less easily distinguished. Children early become acquainted with the distinguishing properties of the things daily offered to their senses, and in a few years find out the characteristick marks of numerous classes of things, and learn the use of language.

24. Things, which have no immediate reference to material objects, such as thoughts, affections, and mental operations, are analyzed in the same manner as objects of sense. The words *abstract* and *reason* denote processes of thought, each of which may be readily distinguished into separate parts, and these parts into others more remote. The same may be said of moral qualities, as justice, prudence, benevolence, and the like. In these, as in sensible objects, there are certain parts, which are instantly noticed, and others, which are discovered by attentive observation. The analysis begins in both cases with the leading

qualities, and becomes more perfect as new qualities are discovered.

25. We employ analysis in interpreting symbolical language and ambiguous propositions. Analysis enables us to investigate causes by their effects, and to find out the means necessary to attain an end proposed, by having the end first in view. It is by this instrument, that the chymist and botanist retrace the processes of nature, and ascertain the qualities of mineral and vegetable substances.

Analysis will be further considered under the head of Inductive Reasoning.*

* Condillac, Logick, part i. Watts, Logick, part iv. ch. 1 Stewart, Elem. vol. ii. ch. 4.

PART SECOND.

OF TERMS AND PROPOSITIONS.

CHAPTER FIRST.
LOGICAL DISTINCTIONS OF TERMS.

26. *Words* possess no natural aptness to denote the particular things, to which they are applied, rather than others, but acquire this aptness wholly by convention. Had the connexion between the name and the thing been established by nature, there would have been but one language in the world. But we find different words employed in different countries, and with equal advantage, to signify the same thing. Thus *white*, *albus*, and *blanc*, denote the same colour. The principal distinctions of terms in logick are the following:

27. First, terms are either *simple* or *complex*. *A simple term is a single word;* as man, horse, tree. *A complex term consists of two or more words, representing some object or association*, formed to be the subject or predicate of a proposition;* as, human fortitude, a swift

---
* See ch. 3.

horse, an amiable deportment. *A word, which denotes several individuals of the same sort, is called a collective term;* as, army, forest, drove.

28. Secondly, terms are distinguished into *absolute* and *relative*. *An absolute term is one, which represents an object or quality, without intimating its relation to any other thing;* as man, river, mountain, roundness, strength. *A relative term denotes an · object so far only as it is connected with some other object.* Thus, *father* implies a man primarily, as 'he is considered the cause of existence to another individual, denominated in reference to him, *son*. These two terms, intimating each other, by a reciprocal reference, are called *correlative*. So *patron* and *client, husband* and *wife, guardian* and *ward,* are correlative terms.

There are other relative terms, as *who, which, it, that,* and the like, which barely recall certain other words, before mentioned; hence the words they refer to are denominated *antecedents*.

29. Thirdly, terms are distinguished into *univocal, equivocal,* and *synonymous*. *Univocal terms are such as have invariably the same signification annexed to them.* Thus *individual-*

ity, *genus*, *electricity*, are univocal terms; for they always signify the same things. *Equivocal words are such as are employed in different senses.* Of this sort is the word *head*, which may signify a part of a nail, of an animal, or of a discourse. So the words *post* and *shore* are equivocal; for they are used in various senses.

That some words should be used in different senses is unavoidable, on account of the scantiness of language, which does not afford a distinct name for every idea. Notwithstanding this, we sometimes find two or more words applied to the same thing; as *wave* and *billow*, *dwelling* and *habitation*. These are called *synonymous* terms.

30. A fourth distinction of terms is into *abstract* and *concrete*. *An abstract term is one, which signifies some quality or attribute, without referring to any subject, in which it may be found;* as roundness, hardness, equality, firmness. *Concrete terms denote both the attributes and the subjects, to which they belong.* Sometimes they express the subjects *directly*, and the attributes *indirectly;* and sometimes the reverse. Thus *philosopher*, *statesman*, *me-*

chanick, are concrete terms, which *directly* denote persons, and *indirectly* the attributes, for which they are distinguished. But *wise, valiant, swift, hard*, are concretes, *immediately* signifying certain attributes, and *indirectly* intimating the persons or things, to which they belong.

31. Fifthly, terms are either *singular* or *universal*. *A singular term is the proper name of some individual person, place, or thing;* as Alexander, London, Danube, Etna. *Proper names* are given only to those things, which we have frequent occasion to mention, as individuals. The design of proper names is to represent these, apart from the classes, to which they belong. Any term, that does this office, is a proper name; and loses not its character as such by being applied, as it frequently is, to several individuals of the same kind, as Peter, John, William.

32. *Universal terms*, otherwise denominated *common* or *appellative, are names indiscriminately applicable to many individual beings*, whether natural or artificial, by reason of certain properties, which they possess in com-

mon. Thus *man, city, river, mountain,* are universal terms, because they agree to all men, cities, rivers, and mountains.

33. Universal terms make the greatest part of the words of every language. Their signification is designedly imperfect; comprising only the most common and obvious properties of things. They are abridgments of language, happily contrived to facilitate and expedite the intercourse of society. Every production of nature and art, and every property of mind and body, is an individual. Each has some properties peculiar to itself; and others, which it possesses in common with many other beings. By discarding the peculiar properties, and retaining under distinct names those, which are common, we reduce to a limited number of classes the innumerable objects, which fall under our observation. This distribution of things into classes forms what logicians call the *genera* and *species* of things.

34. *Species denotes a sort or class, including only individuals; and genus a class including under it two or more species.* A species is formed by applying a name to that property, or collection of properties, in which many

individuals are found to agree. Thus *man* is a species; for the name is applicable to an indefinite number of individual beings, on account of their agreeing in the essential properties of an erect figure, and the faculties of speech and reason. So *horse, deer, eagle, tree,* are species. *Genus* implies the property or properties which different species possess in common. Thus the property of walking on four feet is the foundation of the genus *quadruped,* which applies to *horse, lion, dog, elephant,* and many other species. So *bird* is a genus, of which *eagle, lark, swan,* and *sparrow,* are species.

35. In the distribution of things into genera and species, regard is had to the *comprehension* and *extension* of general terms. By the *comprehension of a term is meant the aggregate of all the known properties of that thing, or class of things,* to which it is applied. Thus *gold* includes in its comprehension a material substance, a yellow colour, superior weight, ductility, fusibility, and every other known property of that body. The *extension of a term regards the number of individual subjects, to which it may be applied.* So the term *gold*

includes in its extension every separate parcel of that metal. *Man* includes in its extension every individual of the human race.

36. Classes are multiplied as the convenience of language is found to require; nature having affixed no limits to the number, that may be formed. As the number of classes increases, the names, which express them, become more complicate in their signification, and less extensive in their application to individuals. Hence it is received as a maxim in logick, that, *as the comprehension of a general term is enlarged, its extension must be diminished; and the contrary*. The comprehension of any species is obviously greater than that of the genus, to which it is subordinate; for the species includes all the attributes of the genus, and others in addition. Thus, in the following subordinate terms, *swallow*, *bird*, *animal*, all the attributes of *bird* are found in *swallow*, and all those of *animal*, in *bird;* but, in each remove, a part of the first collection of attributes is discarded. The case is different with respect to their extension; that of *animal* is much greater than that of *bird*, and that of *bird*, greater than that of *swallow*.

37 The ranks, which lie above any class, or which embrace a wider extension, are called, in reference to it, *superior;* and that, which terminates the series, is called *most general*, or the *highest genus*. Descending from this, each rank is called *inferior;* and the lowest class, which includes only individuals, is called the *lowest species*. All the intermediate ranks, between the highest genus and the lowest species, are termed *subaltern;* each being indifferently either a genus or a species, according as it is considered in the ascending or descending series. Thus *bird* is a genus, when referred to *eagle, raven, sparrow*, but a species, when referred to the more general term, *animal*.

38. *The genus next above any species is called the proximate genus, and any genus above that, a remote genus of that species*. Thus *quadruped* is the proximate, and *animal* a remote genus of *horse*. The property, or collection of properties, by which any species is distinguished from every other species of the same genus, is the *specifick difference*. So *juice* is the proximate genus of *wine;* but the circumstance of being pressed *from grapes* is the

DEFINITION. 39

specifick difference, which distinguishes wine from cider and perry, which are also juices.*

CHAPTER SECOND.

DEFINITION AND DIVISION.

39. *Definitions* are usually distinguished into two kinds; one *nominal*, or of the name; the other *real*, or of the thing. *A definition of the name is merely a specification of the object, to which a name is applied. A definition of the thing is properly an analysis of a thing, or an enumeration of its principal attributes.*

40. Words, which stand for indivisible objects, admit only of nominal definitions. These are sometimes sufficiently explained by intelligible synonymous words; thus *being* denotes existence; *identity* implies sameness. Those, which stand for simple qualities of body, may be defined by referring to the subjects, in which those qualities reside; and those, that denote mental states, by describing the occasions, on which they are produced. Thus *yellow* is the

* Locke, Essay on the Understanding, b. iii. ch. 3. Reid, Essays. vo!. ii. essay v. ch. 1. Belsham, Logick, part i. sect. 4 and 5. Kirwan, Logick, part i. ch. 2, sect. 2.

colour of gold or saffron. *Surprise* is the passion, or state of mind, produced by the perception of some new or uncommon object.

41. A *real definition* leads us to a knowledge of the nature of a thing, by enumerating its most essential modes and properties. Thus a *circle* is a figure, whose circumference is, in every part, equally distant from the centre. *Injustice* is an intentional violation of another's rights. Real definition includes the nominal; for an explanation of the nature of any thing necessarily fixes the signification of the name, by which it is called. Natural substances, and all compound beings, whether real or imaginary, are susceptible of real definitions.

42. Logicians divide a definition into two parts, which are called *genus* and *difference.* If the thing to be defined be in any degree general, that is, expressed by a generick term, the definition will be made up of the proxi mate genus and the specifick difference. Thus *bird* is an animal, which has wings, feathers, and a hard, glossy bill. *Animal* is the proxi mate genus, denoting what *bird* has in common with *horse, deer, elephant;* the other terms denote the specifick difference; for they

point out the properties, which distinguish *bird* from every other species of animals. So *square* is a figure, which has four equal sides, and four right angles. *Figure* is the proximate genus; the other terms make the specifick difference.

43. If the thing to be defined be an individual, having a proper name, the definition will consist of the species and an enumeration of so many properties, as will distinguish that individual from all others of that species. Thus *Mercury* is the planet nearest the sun. *Planet* is the lowest species; *nearest the sun* is the circumstance, which sufficiently marks a difference between Mercury and the other planets.

45. There are many words in every lan guage, which cannot be defined, because they have no uniform signification affixed to them. *The, this, that, which, such, every, good, bad, desirable*, and the like, are nearly insignificant sounds, till they are applied to particular things, from which they borrow a sort of local or temporary meaning; and they often signify different things, when applied to different subjects. *Good*, applied to a soldier, means

courage ; to a Christian, piety ; to a physician, skill; to a horse, strength; to a knife, sharpness.

45. Words of this description, which have no uniform signification affixed to them, are wholly employed in the definition of other terms. The definitive particles have no other use, than to restrain the latitude of general terms. For example, *the* man, *this* horse, *that* tree, *such* an object. Here the names *man, horse, tree,* and *object,* which represent whole classes of things, are restrained by the words *the, this, that,* and *such,* to certain individuals, with which we are supposed to be already acquainted.

Again, a *wide* river, a *severe* winter, a *delightful* prospect. The terms *river, winter,* and *prospect,* are general; *wide, severe,* and *delightful,* denote specifick differences. Wherever the latitude of a general word is restrained by a definitive, or a quality is attributed to a subject, we may recognise the two essential parts of a definition, namely, genus and difference.

46. *Division is the explication of any whole by the enumeration of its component parts.* Thus a *tree* is divided into trunk, roots, and

branches; *animal*, into beast, bird, fish, and insect. The term, *division*, is applicable to the resolution of a treatise or discourse into its several heads or branches; also, to the consideration of an equivocal word in reference to its different significations.

The members of a division should exhaust the subject divided; and they should be so opposed, that one will not be contained in another. The parts, into which any thing is first divided, should be the largest and most general. The resolution of one of these parts into others, more minute, is called *subdivision*. So a year is first divided into months. Month is then subdivided into weeks; week, into days, and so on. Needless subdivisions should be avoided, as they burden the memory, and introduce confusion.*

CHAPTER THIRD.

GENERAL DESCRIPTION OF PROPOSITIONS.

17. *A proposition is a verbal representation of some perception, act, or affection of the mind.*

* Locke, Essay, b. iii. Watts, Logick, part i. Kirwan, Logick, part 1.

The constituent parts of a proposition are the *subject*, the *predicate*, and the *copula*. The two first are called *terms*, because they are the extremes of the proposition; and they may consist of a single word each, or of a collection of words, representing some person, thing, or attribute.

48. *The subject of a proposition is that, concerning which something is either asserted, denied, commanded, or inquired. The predicate is that, which is asserted, denied, commanded, or inquired, concerning the subject. The copula is that, by which the other two parts are connected.*

> Body is divisible.
> Man is not omniscient.
> Be ye filled.
> Is Cæsar dead ?

Body, man, ye, and *Cæsar*, are the subjects of these four propositions; *divisible, omniscient, filled,* and *dead,* are the predicates; *is, is not,* and *be,* the copulas. In the first example, the agreement between the subject and predicate is asserted; in the second, it is denied; in the third, it is ordered; in the fourth, it is inquired for.

49. One part of a proposition is often contained in another. In the following examples, the copula is contained in the predicate.

> I think.
> The sun rises.

These imply,

> I am thinking.
> The sun is rising.

So the copula sometimes includes the whole, or a part of the predicate; as, Troy was; that is, Troy was *existent*. The copula is always some inflection of the verb *to be*, either expressed or understood.

A single word may contain a complete proposition. Thus *scribo* implies *ego sum scribens*, I am writing. So *rejoice, attend*, imply *be thou rejoicing ; be thou attentive*.

50. The subject of the proposition usually stands first, and the predicate last; but this order is sometimes inverted, as in the following example:

> In China are many ingenious artists.

That is,

> Many ingenious artists are [existent] in China.

The words, which constitute the two terms, are sometimes so blended together, that the whole, or a part, of one is placed between parts of the other. In the following example, the whole subject intervenes between parts of the predicate:

"But too often different is *rational conjecture* from melancholy fact." *Burke.*

In imperative and interrogative propositions, the copula is usually placed first. As,

>Be thou faithful.
>Is the controversy settled?

51. *An identical proposition is one, whose subject and predicate are composed of the same word or words, and express precisely the same idea.* Sometimes the terms are the same, and the ideas different. Thus, *home is home.* This proposition is not identical; for *home*, as subject, means only a place of residence; but as predicate, it denotes that it is an agreeable residence. Sometimes the terms are different, but express the same idea. Thus, *three times three are nine; twelve is the fifth part of sixty.* Here the terms are reciprocal, and may be substituted for each other; but the propositions are not strictly identical.

CHAPTER FOURTH.

SIMPLE, COMPLEX, AND MODAL PROPOSITIONS.

52. *A simple proposition is one, whose subject and predicate are composed of simple terms.* [See No. 27.] As,

> Time is precious.
> Virtue will be rewarded.

A complex proposition has one or both of its terms complex. They are formed in different ways. A proposition is sometimes rendered complex, by having for its subject or predicate some other proposition, or words equivalent. Thus,

> That one man should be punished for the crimes of another is unjust.

The words, which precede *is*, and which form the subject of this example, obviously contain an entire proposition.

53. Frequently the subject of a proposition is first represented by the pronoun *it*, and afterwards distinctly expressed; as in the following expression:

> "It is impossible to guess at the term to which our forbearance would have extended."[*]

[*] Burke, Regicide Peace.

The words, constituting the real subject, are here represented by the word *it*, which being discarded, and the subject stated first, the proposition will stand thus:

> To guess at the term, to which our forbearance would have extended, is impossible.

54. Another manner of rendering a proposition complex is by introducing the pronoun *who*, *which*, or *that*, for the purpose of explaining the subject or predicate. Thus,

> Cyrus, who founded the Persian empire, was the son of Cambyses.

The words, introduced by the relative, form a complete proposition, which is called the *incident;* and the whole proposition, including this, is called, in reference to it, *primary* or *principal*. As the design of the incident proposition is purely to explain the subject or predicate of the primary, it can be considered only as a part of the term, in which it is placed.

55. Lastly, any proposition is complex, whose subject or predicate is defined, by annexing to it a word of limitation, or restriction. As,

> *Upright* men are respected.
> The mind is a *simple* substance.

The subject of the first example is defined by the word *upright;* and the predicate of the second, by the word *simple*. These words restrain the latitude of the general terms, *men* and *substance*, to which they are joined. They are equivalent to incidental propositions, and may be readily resolved into them. Thus,

> Men who are upright, are respected.
> The mind is a substance, that is simple.

56. *A modal proposition is one, whose copula is qualified by some word or words, representing the manner of the agreement or discrepancy between the subject and predicate.* The modality of propositions is frequently expressed by the auxiliary verbs, *may, can, must, ought*, and the like, which imply possibility, necessity, or contingency. Thus,

> Men of influence *can* do much good.
> Subordination *must* be maintained.

The thing asserted, in each of these propositions, is not the simple and absolute agreement of the subject with the predicate, but barely the nature of that agreement; namely, that it is possible or necessary.*

CHAPTER FIFTH.

QUALITY AND QUANTITY OF PROPOSITIONS.

57. Propositions are further distinguished into *affirmative* and *negative;* which has been called a distinction with respect to *quality*. In *affirmative propositions, the predicate and subject are asserted to agree*. As,

Clovis was the founder of the French monarchy.

In *negative propositions, the predicate is declared to be incompatible with the subject*. This is commonly done by placing the negative particle *not* immediately after the copula. Thus,

The world is *not* eternal.

58. Sometimes the negative particle is placed so far from the copula, that it appears to have no immediate connexion with it; but rather to belong to some other part of the proposition :

Not all the troops united were able to defend the fortress.

---

* Watts, Logick, part ii. ch. 2. Kirwan, Logick, part 1. ch. 2.

Here the negative word is placed before the subject; but still its influence falls wholly on the copula, and makes the proposition signify the opposite of what it would without it. This will be made evident by stating the proposition thus,

All the troops united were *not* able to defend the fortress.

59. By the *quantity* of a proposition is meant its consideration in respect to the extent of its subject; and according as the subject is used in the whole or a part of its extension, propositions are denominated *universal* or *particular*. *A universal proposition is one, whose subject is a general term, used in the whole of its extension.* The signs of universality are *all*, *each*, *every*, *no*, *neither*, and the like. Thus,

All free agents are accountable.
Every sin is a violation of the Divine law.

These are universal propositions; because each subject includes an extensive class, to each individual of which the predicate is declared applicable.

60. When the sign of universality is omitted, or the indefinite article is placed before

the general subject, the proposition is called *indefinite*. Thus,

> Planets are continually changing their places.
> A just sovereign regards the welfare of his subjects.

These subjects are taken in their greatest extent; for if there were any planet, that did not change its place, or any just sovereign, who neglected the welfare of his subjects, the proposition would not be true.

61. *A particular proposition is one, whose subject is a general term, but is taken only in a part of its extension.* The signs of particularity are *some, many, most, several, few*, and the like.

> Some animals are amphibious.
> Many buildings were destroyed.

The words, *some* and *many*, restrain the subjects, *animals* and *buildings*, and intimate, that a part only of the individual beings, which they include, will admit the predicates, *amphibious* and *destroyed*.

62. A proposition, whose subject is the proper name of some individual person or thing, is denominated *singular*. As,

Alfred founded the University of Oxford.
Stagira was the birthplace of Aristotle.

A definitive pronoun, placed before the subject of a proposition, renders it singular. As,

That general was defeated.

The subject of a singular proposition, as it represents only an individual, is necessarily taken in its whole extension; for which reason singular propositions are classed with universal. Every proposition, therefore, is either universal or particular.

63. Besides this quantity in the subject, there is another quality in the predicate of a proposition; for this, as well as the subject, is taken either in the whole, or only in a part of its extension. The quantity of the subject and that of the proposition are the same; for *in every universal proposition, the subject is universal; and in every particular proposition, the subject is particular*. But the quantity of the predicate depends on the quality of the proposition. [See No. 57.] *In an affirmative proposition the predicate is particular; and in all negative propositions it is universal.*

64. The predicate of an affirmative proposition, separately considered, is commonly a more general term than the subject. It is usually a genus, of which the subject is a species. But, when united to the subject, no greater extension is attributed to it than is just sufficient to enable it to embrace the subject. It is taken in the whole of its comprehension, but in a part only of its extension. [See No. 35.] For example,

Every dog is an animal.

Here it is barely asserted, that the predicate, *animal*, does extend so far as to include every individual of the subject, *dog;* but it is neither asserted nor denied, that it is susceptible of a greater extension. Now, though the term, *animal*, separately considered, is applicable to millions of beings besides dogs, still, in this place, it has no more extension than is expressly given it by the words of the proposition. The predicate of every affirmative proposition being in this way restrained by its subject, universality can never be attributed to it.

65. But in negative propositions, the predicate, not being restrained by a subject, to which

it is declared inapplicable, is taken in the whole of its extension. Thus,

> No animal is a tree.

This proposition implies, that the things, included under *tree*, are so dissimilar to those, included under *animal*, that no individual can be found, to which the two terms will apply.

CHAPTER SIXTH.
OPPOSITION AND CONVERSION OF PROPOSITIONS.

66. *Opposition in propositions implies a disagreement in respect of quality.* Two propositions, which have the same subject and the same predicate, are said to be opposite, when one absolutely denies, in whole or in part, what the other affirms. There are three ways, in which propositions of this sort may be opposed. First, a universal affirmative may be opposed to a particular negative. These are called *contradictory*. As,

> Every defensive war is just.
> Some defensive wars are not just.

Secondly, a universal affirmative proposition may oppose a universal negative. These are called *contrary*. As,

Every disease is contagious.
No disease is contagious.

Thirdly, a particular affirmative may be opposed to a particular negative. These are called *subcontrary*. As,

Some amusements are innocent.
Some amusements are not innocent.

Two contradictory propositions can never be either both true, or both false, at the same time; two contraries may be both false, but they cannot be both true; and two subcontraries may be both true, but they cannot be both false, at the same time.

67. *The conversion of a proposition is the transposition of its terms, so that the subject shall take the place of the predicate, and the predicate the place of the subject, with the preservation of truth.* When the subject and predicate simply change places, without causing any alteration in the quantity of the propositions, it is called a *simple conversion*. But if, in the new arrangement, a term of particularity is introduced, to restrain the subject of the derivative proposition within the same extension, which it had as predicate of the original, this is called a *particular conversion;* by the schoolmen it was

OF PROPOSITIONS. 57

denominated *conversio per accidens*. Universal affirmative propositions are usually convertible only in the latter mode; but universal negatives and particular affirmatives are convertible in the former.

68. The converse of a universal affirmative proposition must, generally speaking,* be a particular affirmative. It is necessary that both the terms be taken in exactly the same extension, in both arrangements; and since, by the rule stated in No. 63, the predicate of the original proposition must be particular, this same term must be particular in the converse, where it is made the subject, which will therefore render the proposition particular. Thus

>*Orig. Prop.* All swallows are birds.
>*Converse.* Some birds are swallows.

69. The converse of a universal negative proposition is a universal negative. The subject and predicate, being of equal extent, mutually exclude each other; and as these terms

---

* This is always the case, except in those propositions, whose predicate is a complete definition of the subject. In such propositions, the subject and predicate are reciprocal terms. As, *four times five are twenty;* and *twenty are four times five*. *Wine is the juice of the grape;* and *the juice of the grape is wine*.

are both universal in the first arrangement, [See No. 65,] they must be so in the second. Thus,

Orig. Prop. No deer is an elephant.
Converse. No elephant is a deer.

70. Particular affirmative propositions are convertible only into the same. In these the terms are both particular; [See No. 61, 63;] and they can never become otherwise by a new arrangement. Thus,

Orig. Prop. Some birds lie dormant during the winter.
Converse. Some beings, that lie dormant during the winter, are birds.

71. A particular negative proposition is inconvertible in any mode. Its subject is particular, and by conversion this subject would be made the predicate of a negative proposition, and must therefore be universal, according to No. 65; a whole deduced from a part, which is impossible. For example; from this proposition,

Some birds are not swallows,

we cannot affirm this,

No swallows are birds.

This would be to deduce a whole from a part;

since *swallow* is denied of a part only of the extension of *bird*, in the first proposition; and of the whole of it, in the last.*

72. There is a third species of conversion, in which a negative particle is inserted both in the subject and predicate of the derivative proposition, unless previously included in the original. This is denominated conversion by *contraposition.* Thus,

Orig. Prop. Every bird is an animal.
Converse. That, which is not an animal, is not a bird.

These negatives destroy each other, and the proposition is considered as affirmative.†

CHAPTER SEVENTH.

COMPOUND PROPOSITIONS.

73. *A compound proposition is one, which has two or more subjects, or predicates, or both; and may be resolved into two or more propositions.*

---

* In a universal affirmative proposition, the subject only is universal, and the predicate particular; in a universal negative, the subject and predicate are both universal; in a particular affirmative, the subject and predicate are both particular; and in a particular negative, the subject only is particular, and the predicate universal.
† Watts, Logick, part ii. ch. 2. Kirwan, Logick, part i. ch. 3

As,

Spring, summer, autumn, and winter, are seasons of the year.

Alfred was prudent, valiant, just, and benevolent.

As the four subjects of the first example are separately applicable to the predicate, *seasons of the year*, and the four predicates of the last, separately applicable to the subject, *Alfred*, each may be resolved into four propositions. Thus,

>Spring is a season of the year.
>Summer is a season of the year, &c.

74. Every compound proposition may be reduced to as many single ones as it contains subjects, to which the whole predicate will apply, and predicates, to which the whole subject will apply; or as there are parts in each, which are separately applicable to each other.

Beasts, birds, and insects, have life, sense, and motion.

This example contains three subjects and three predicates, and may be reduced to nine distinct propositions.

75. Two or more words are sometimes so coupled together in the subject or predicate, as to give the proposition the appearance of

being compound, when it is single. Thus,

> Joy and sorrow are opposite qualities.
> Ye cannot serve God and Mammon.

These are complex propositions, but they are not compound; for neither of them can be resolved into two propositions. The two parts, which make up respectively the subject of the one and the predicate of the other, must be taken conjointly.

76. Compound propositions may be distinguished from those, that are barely complex, by the following circumstances. First, in a compound proposition, the parts, which constitute the subject or predicate, are independent of each other, and may be taken separately, as well as conjointly; which is not the case in complex propositions. In the latter, either certain words are joined together, which represent integral parts of some whole, that is to be the subject or predicate, as *three and seven are equal to ten;* or one part of the proposition is repeated, directly or implicitly, by some relative word, as, *it, that, who which;* or, lastly, the real subject or predicate is defined by an explanatory word. In either of these cases,

the words, which render the proposition complex, must be regarded as real parts of the term, in which they occur.

77. Secondly, wherever a complex proposition involves a simple one, there will be the distinction of primary and incidental; and the incidental proposition may be false, while the primary is true. But, in compound propositions, there exists no distinction of primary and incidental, each part being independent of the rest; and the compound proposition must be false, when any one of the propositions, it involves, is false, though the others be true.

78. Compound propositions are, in most books of logick, distributed into various sorts, denominated *copulative, disjunctive, conditional, causal, relative,* and *discretive;* which denominations are taken from the particle, employed in the composition of their subject or predicate. The examples, already given, belong to the first class.

A disjunctive proposition asserts, that a subject agrees with one of two or more named predicates, or a predicate with one of two or more subjects enumerated; but does not specify which.

Thus,

Either the sun or the moon will be eclipsed, on Christmas day,

The weather will, at that time, be either clear or cloudy.

79. *A discretive proposition consists of two parts, which are contrasted by reason of some apparent opposition or inconsistency, intimated by the particles* but, though, notwithstanding, *and the like.* As,

Hannibal, *though* unfortunate, was a great general.

A man may deceive his neighbor, *but* not his God

80. The other distinctions of this class are incorrect. What are usually termed *conditional, causal,* and *relative* propositions, are nothing more than different modes of connecting two entire propositions together. It is essential to the individuality of a proposition, that it have but one copula. However compounded or complicated the subject or predicate may be, they must be connected by a single affirmation or negation. This rule is violated in every instance of what are called conditional, causal, and relative propositions. The following have been given as examples of these kinds:

If the sun be fixed, the earth must move.

Rehoboam was unhappy, *because* he followed evil counsel.

As is the Father, *so* is the Son.

The first is given as an example of a *conditional*, the second, of a *causal*, and the third, of a *relative* proposition. But no one of them can, with any propriety, be considered as a compound proposition. Each example consists of two entire propositions, possessing distinct subjects, copulas, and predicates; and so put together as to constitute a complete act of ratiocination.*

---

* Collard, Logick, part iii. ch. 2. Kirwan, Logick, part i. ch. 4; Watts, Logick, part ii. ch. 2.

PART THIRD.

OF JUDGMENT AND REASONING.

CHAPTER FIRST.

INTUITIVE EVIDENCE.

81. *Judgment is an act of the mind, uniting or separating two objects of thought according as they are perceived to agree or disagree.* The relation between these objects is sometimes discovered by barely contemplating them, without reference to any thing else; and sometimes by comparing them with other objects, to which they have a known relation. The former is simple comparison; the latter is an act of reasoning. The determination of the mind in both cases is denominated *judgment.* Every act of judgment is grounded on some sort of evidence. That, which determines the mind in simple comparison, is called *intuitive evidence;* and that, which is employed in reasoning *deductive.*

The principal kinds of intuitive evidence, or sources of intuitive belief, are the evidence of *sense*, of *consciousness*, of *memory*, and of *axioms*, or *general principles*.

82. The first source of intuitive belief is the *testimony of the external senses*, hearing, seeing, touching, smelling, and tasting. These organs come to their usual degree of maturity in infancy, and are employed with equal confidence by all descriptions of people. Men have, in every country, and in every period of the world, been governed by their testimony, even in their most important concerns. We can no more question the existence of the bodies, which we see and handle, than we can our own existence, or the truth of the most obvious maxim, that can be proposed to our thoughts. On the evidence of the senses is grounded all our knowledge of the nature, powers, and qualities of the material objects around us. All truths relative to physical science or to the events of history, and all those rules of prudence, which relate to the preservation and health of our bodies, must ultimately be resolved into this principle, that things are as our senses represent them.

83. *Consciousness* is another source of intuitive evidence. Its office is to inform us of the present existence of our various passions, affections, and mental operations. The whole science of the human mind is built on this evidence; and no branch of knowledge stands on a surer foundation; for no evidence is superior to this, where it is completely ascertained. But it is sometimes difficult to define precisely the subjects of our consciousness. Those, who have not been accustomed to attend to their intellectual operations, are liable to err in applying this evidence. I think, compare, reason, doubt; I feel pain, or pleasure; I remember past events. These are facts, of which I am conscious, and of which I am unable to question the reality. The power of consciousness is exercised but imperfectly, till the mind advances towards maturity. Some[*] have supposed it to be wholly dormant during the years of childhood. It is however exercised, in a greater or less degree, by people of all classes; and the subjects, about which it is employed, can be no other than the mental states of a being, which each one calls *himself*

[*] Scott, Intellectual Philosophy.

84. As the evidence of sense furnishes us with the knowledge of things present in the material world, and the evidence of consciousness informs us of whatever is passing in our own minds; so the evidence of *memory* gives us immediate knowledge of things past, whether of a material or intellectual kind. This evidence has ever commanded the belief of mankind as effectually as that of sense. Past facts and occurrences, of which we have a clear remembrance, are regarded as certain. This is implied by men in all their efforts to gather knowledge and improvement from their past experience. It is on this principle, that causes, which involve the lives and fortunes of men, are decided by the testimony of witnesses, in courts of justice. Propositions, formerly proved, may be relied on as present knowledge, though the reasons, which first gained our assent to them, be now forgotten, provided we remember that we once carefully investigated them, and were then certain of their truth. Such propositions must often be introduced or referred to in demonstrations; and, should doubts be entertained respecting their truth, they must weaken our confidence in the con-

clusions, to which they are subservient. Unless therefore the evidence of memory be admitted as a ground of certain knowledge, the foundation of demonstrative reasoning would be destroyed.

85. Another species of intuitive evidence is that, which accompanies *mathematical axioms* and all those abstract truths, which carry their own evidence with them, and are readily assented to, as soon as they are contemplated. Thus, *the whole is greater than a part. Things equal to the same are equal to one another. Every effect must have a cause.* These propositions force our assent by irresistible evidence, as soon as we understand the terms, by which they are expressed. They cannot be proved; because no principles more evident can be assumed, from which their truth could be deduced. In all demonstrative reasoning, constant use is made of these abstract and self-evident propositions.*

* Beattie, Essay on Truth, part i. ch. 2. Stewart, Elem. vol. ii. ch 1. Campbell, Phil. Rhet. vol. i. ch. 5. Scott, Elem. Intel. Phil. ch. 8, sect. 3.

CHAPTER SECOND.

DIFFERENCE BETWEEN MORAL AND DEMONSTRATIVE REASONING.

86. *Reasoning is a process, by which unknown truths are inferred from those, which are already known or admitted.* The evidence, employed in reasoning, is *deductive*, and is distinguished into two kinds, which are, *moral* and *demonstrative*. *Moral evidence is that species of proof, which is employed on subjects, directly or indirectly connected with moral conduct.* It is not however confined to such subjects; but is extended to all those facts and events, concerning which we do not obtain the evidence of sense, intuition, or demonstration; and to all the general truths, which are deduced from observation and experience.* *Demonstrative evidence is that, by which we trace the relations, subsisting among things, in their nature immutable, like the subjects of geometry and arithmetick.* On this distinction of deduc tive evidence is founded the most general divi sion of reasoning, which is into *moral* or *proba*

---

* Gambier, Moral Evidence, ch. 1.

ble, and *demonstrative.* The principal differences in these modes of reasoning are the following:

87. First, they differ in regard to their subjects. Demonstration is employed about abstract and independent truths, or those relations, which are considered as necessary, and whose subjects may be exactly measured and defined. The properties of number and quantity are of this sort. They have no respect to time or place; depend on no cause; and are subject to no change. But the subjects of moral reasoning are matters of fact, which are in their nature contingent, and the variable connexions, which subsist among things in actual existence. Thus, that *mercury may be congealed by cold*, that *lead is fusible*, *that Hannibal led an army over the Alps*, that *Lisbon was once destroyed by an earthquake*, and the like, are truths within the province of moral reasoning.

88. Secondly. In a demonstration, it is not necessary to examine more than one side of the question; for if any proposition be demonstrated to be true, whatever can be offered, as proof, on the opposite side, must be mere fallacy. But in cases of moral reasoning, there

are frequently arguments of weight on both sides; and therefore, in order to judge correctly, we must consider each side of the question, and give our assent to that, on which there appears the greatest weight of evidence. Thus, having demonstrated *the quality of the three angles of a triangle to two right ones*, there is no need of inquiring what may be urged against the demonstration. But the case is different in questions of a moral kind, as *whether falsehood may be practised towards an assassin;* or *whether an oath, extorted by violence, be obligatory.* In such questions, the mind is often perplexed, and the judgment held in suspense by the conflict of opposite reasons.

89. Thirdly. Propositions, contrary to those established by moral evidence, are merely *false;* but those, which are contrary to demonstrated propositions, are not only false, but likewise *absurd.* Thus, the assertion, that *Carthage was never taken by the Romans* though false, is not absurd; for there was a time, when it was true. But the assertion, that *the opposite angles, formed by two straight*

lines crossing each other, are not equal, is not only false, but also absurd.

90. Fourthly. In demonstration there are no degrees; the conclusion resulting necessarily from the definitions and principles, which have been assumed as the basis of the reasoning. But in moral reasoning there is often contrariety of evidence; and the degree of assurance, we feel in the conclusion, must depend on the degree, in which the evidence on one side exceeds that on the other.

91. Fifthly. In every process of demonstrative reasoning, the proofs are framed into one coherent series, each part of which must have an intuitive agreement with that, which goes before, and with that, which follows it. The longest geometrical demonstration is but one uniform chain, the links of which, taken separately, are not regarded as so many arguments; and consequently, when thus taken, they prove nothing. But taken together, and in their proper order, they form one argument, which is perfectly conclusive. In a process of moral reasoning, on the contrary, there is usually a combination of many separate arguments, in no degree dependent on each other. Each

possesses some weight, and bestows on the conclusion a certain degree of probability; of all which, accumulated, the credibility of the fact is compounded. Thus the proof, that *the Romans once possessed Great Britain*, is made up of a variety of independent arguments: as, immemorial tradition: the testimony of historians; the ruins of Roman buildings, camps, and walls; Roman coins, inscriptions, and the like. These are independent arguments; but they all conspire to establish the fact.

92. Sixthly. It may be further noticed, that the obstacles, which occur in the practice of these two modes of reasoning, are of different kinds. Those, which impede our progress in demonstration, arise from the large number of intermediate steps, and the difficulty of finding suitable media of proof. In moral reasoning, the processes are usually short, and the chief obstacles, by which we are retarded, arise from the want of exact definitions to our words; the difficulty of keeping steadily in view the various circumstances, on which our judgment should be formed; and from the prejudices arising from early impressions and associations.

93. It should be remarked here, that the epithet *probable*, as applied by logicians to the evidence of moral reasoning, has a technical meaning, altogether different from its usual signification. In common discourse, it is applied to evidence, which does not command a full assent; but in logical discussions, it has a more comprehensive meaning, not only including every *subordinate* degree of moral evidence, but also the *highest*. In this latter sense, it is not to be considered as implying any *deficiency* of proof, but as contradistinguishing one species of proof from another;—not as opposed to what is certain, but to what may be demonstrated after the manner of mathematicians; not as denoting the *degree* of evidence, but its *nature*. It is the more important to keep in mind this distinction between the popular and technical meaning of the term *probable*, as the neglect or misapprehension of it has given origin to a distrust of moral reasoning, as inferior in evidence to mathematical demonstration; and induced many authors to seek for a mode of proof altogether unattainable in moral inquiries,

and which, if it could be attained, would not be less liable to the cavils of scepticks.*

CHAPTER THIRD.

INDUCTION.

94. The first kind of moral reasoning is that, by which we infer general truths from particular facts, that have fallen under our observation. This has been called the method of *induction*. It is founded on the belief, that the course of nature is governed by uniform laws and that things will happen in future, as we have observed them to happen in time past. We can have no proof of a permanent connexion between any events, or between any two qualities either of body or mind. The only reason for supposing such a connexion in any instance is, that we have *invariably* found certain things to have been conjoined in fact; and this experience, in many cases, produces a conviction equal to that of demonstration.

95. When a property has been found in

* Reid, Intellectual Powers, essay vii. ch. 2. Campbell, Phil. Rhet. b. i. ch. 5. sect. 2. Gambier, Mor. Evid. ch. 1. Stewart, Elem. Phil. of Mind, vol. i. Introd. part ii. sect. 2. vol. ii. ch. 2. sect. 4.

in any subjects of a similar kind, and no contradictory instance has been discovered, though diligently sought, we have an irresistible persuasion, that the same property belongs to all the individuals of that class. Thus, having applied a magnet to several masses of iron, and found uniformly a strong attraction to take place, we feel no doubt, that it belongs to the nature of iron to be thus affected by that substance; and, though our experience reaches only to a small part of the masses of iron in existence, we assert with confidence, that all iron is susceptible of magnetical attraction. So, having often noticed, that, by the application of heat to a certain degree, water is made to boil, and that, in the absence of heat to a certain degree, it becomes congealed; and having ascertained these changes to be uniform, so far as they have been observed by ourselves and others, we readily ascribe them to the nature of water, and conclude, that in every country water will boil or freeze, on being exposed to those opposite degrees of temperature.

96. In this way, by observations and experiments on individuals of a similar kind, noticing with exactness their agreement, or the circum-

stances, in which they differ, we obtain general truths relating to the properties and laws of material objects. By the same inductive process we investigate the laws, which govern the phenomena of mind. Thus, from experience, it has been ascertained, that, when two ideas have been often presented to the mind in immediate succession, they acquire a tendency mutually to suggest each other; so that, when either of them occurs to our thoughts, the other readily follows it. We learn also from experience, that the durability of past impressions on the mind depends greatly on the attention, with which they were at first received. From the uniformity of these facts we are taught, that *contiguity in time or place is a principle of association;* and that *attention is necessary to memory.*

97. As we deduce the common properties of a single class of beings from observations on individuals of that class, so, by comparing individuals of different classes, we discover important resemblances between one species and another, and are enabled to obtain more extensive conclusions. Thus, having seen the milk of several animals of different species, and

found it uniformly to be white, we conclude, that the milk of all animals is so. In like manner, having witnessed the effect of fire on several pieces of *gold*, *iron*, *lead*, and so forth, we affirm that all metals are fusible. In this way, beginning with individuals, we ascend to species; and thence proceed from less general to more general conclusions, till we arrive at those abstract propositions, which are called *axioms* or *general truths*.

98. This method of induction is recommended by Lord Bacon, as the first and most important instrument of reason, in its search after truth. We employ it not only in the investigation of general truths, relating to things in actual existence; but in gaining those practical rules and maxims, by which the common business of life is carried on.

99. The use of induction, in learning the signification of words, is thus happily explained by Mr. Stewart: " A familiar illustration of " this process presents itself in the expedient, ' which a reader naturally employs for deci- " phering the meaning of an unknown word, in " a foreign language, when he happens not to " have a dictionary at hand. The first sen-

"tence, where the word occurs, affords, it is "probable, sufficient foundation for a vague "conjecture concerning the notion, annexed "to it by the author; some idea or other being "necessarily substituted in its place, in order "to make the passage at all intelligible. The "next sentence, where it is involved, renders "this conjecture a little more definite; a third "sentence contracts the field of doubt within "still narrower limits; till at length a more "extensive induction fixes completely the sig- "nification we are in quest of. There cannot "be a doubt, I apprehend, that it is in some "such way as this, that children slowly and "imperceptibly enter into the abstract and com- "plex notions, annexed to numberless words in "their mother tongue, of which we should "find it difficult, or impossible, to convey the ' sense by formal definitions."*

100. In another place, Mr. Stewart has described the manner of using induction, in tracing an event to its *physical cause:* " As "we can, in no instance, perceive the link, by "which two successive events are connected, so

---

* Philosophical Essays, essay v. ch. 1.

"as to deduce, by reasoning *a priori*, the one "from the other, as a consequence or effect, "it follows that, when we see an event take "place, which has been preceded by a com- "bination of different circumstances, it is im- "possible for human sagacity to ascertain, "whether the effect is connected with *all* the "circumstances, or only with a part of them; "and, on the latter supposition, which of the "circumstances is essential to the result, and "which are merely accidental accessories or "concomitants. The only way, in such a case, "of coming at the truth, is to repeat over the "experiment again and again, leaving out all "the different circumstances successively, and "observing with what particular combinations "of them the effect is conjoined.

"When, by thus comparing a number of "cases, agreeing in some circumstances, but "differing in others, and all attended with the "same result, a philosopher connects, as a "general law of nature, the event with its "*physical cause*, he is said to proceed according "to the method of *induction*."*

---

* Elements of the Philosophy of the Mind, vol. ii. ch. 4, sec. 1.

101. Inductive conclusions will amount to moral certainty, whenever our experience has been uniform, and the number of cases examined sufficiently numerous. But this reasoning is liable to be fallacious through impatience in the investigation, by which judgments are hastily formed, without a sufficient accumulation of facts. The number of instances, required to justify a general conclusion, must be increased in proportion as the facts, from which we reason, are more irregular in their appearance. In judging concerning the properties of inanimate matter, a general inference may sometimes be drawn from a small number of particular cases. If, for example, *aqua fortis* has been known to dissolve *silver* in one instance, the presumption is very strong, that it will do so in all. But the success, which may happen to attend a medicine in a single instance, furnishes but a slight presumption with regard to its general operation on the human body.

102. When our experience has not been uniform, the conclusions we make will fall short of moral certainty. An equal number of favourable and unfavourable instances leaves the mind in a state of suspense, without exciting

the smallest expectation on either side. As the ratio, which the instances on the two sides bear to each other, may vary indefinitely, so must the judgments, founded on them, vary in a like degree from the neighborhood of certainty, down to that of entire improbability.*

CHAPTER FOURTH.

ANALOGY.

103. Analogy is the foundation of another species of moral reasoning, similar in most respects to analytical induction. They both proceed on the same general principle, that nature is consistent and uniform in her operations; so that from similar circumstances similar effects may be expected; and in proportion as the resemblance between two cases diminishes, the less confidence must be placed in the conclusions, made from the one to the other. The word *analogy* is used with much vagueness. Sometimes it denotes only a slight and distant

---

* Bacon, Novum Oganum, lib. i. Campbell, Phil. Rhet. vol. L. ch. 5, sect 2. Beattie, Essay on Truth, part i. ch. 2, sect. 6. Tatham, Chart and Scale of Truth, vol. i. ch. 4, sect. 1. Stewart, Elem. vol. ii. ch. 4. Gambier, Mor. Evidence, ch 2. Scott, Int'l Phil. Appendix, ch. 2.

resemblance; as that, which is found between different species of the same genus. Sometimes it implies a correspondence of different relations; as that, which exists between the fins of a fish and the wings of a bird; the latter bearing the same relation to the air, that the former does to the water.

104. Inductive and analogical reasoning are so similar in their nature, that it is not easy to point out their specifick difference. Every inductive process commences with analogy. The following circumstances appear to mark a distinction between them, sufficient to justify their being treated as separate articles. First, induction is a process from several individuals of a class to the whole. Its conclusions therefore are always general. But by analogy we argue from one individual being to another of the same class; and from one species to another. Secondly, the evidence, employed in analogy, is wholly *indirect* and *collateral;*—the coexistence of two qualities in one subject affording no direct evidence of their coexistence in any other. But in the inductive process we have direct evidence, that the property, which we apply to a whole class, exists in many individ-

mals of that class. It is true, that in all induction analogy must be used; for we can never separately examine every individual of a whole class, however cautiously we may proceed. So far as we extend our observations or experiments, the evidence is direct; but, with regard to the remaining subjects of the class, the conclusions must rest wholly on analogy.

105. Analogy is an unsafe ground of reasoning; and its conclusions should seldom be received, without some degree of distrust. When things resemble each other in several important circumstances, we are apt to suppose the similitude more extensive than it really is. The ancient anatomists, being hindered by their superstition from dissecting the bodies of men, endeavoured to obtain the information, which might thence have been derived, from those quadrupeds, whose internal structure was thought to approach nearest to that of the human body. In this way they were led into numerous mistakes, which have been detected by the anatomists of modern times.

106. The following is stated by Dr. Reid as an example of analogical reasoning: "We "observe a great similitude between this earth,

"which we inhabit, and the other planets
"Saturn, Jupiter, and so forth. They all re-
"volve round the sun, as the earth does;
"though at different distances and in different
"periods. They borrow all their light from the
"sun, as the earth does. Several of them are
"known to revolve round their axes, like the
"earth, and by that means must have a like
"succession of day and night. Some of them
"have moons, that serve to give them light,
"in the absence of the sun, as our moon does
"to us. They are all in their motions subject
"to the same law of gravitation as the earth
"is. From all this similitude it is not unrea-
"sonable to think, that those planets may,
"like our earth, be the habitation of various
"orders of living creatures."*

In the same manner we may conclude from analogy, that the comets are inhabited. But this conclusion is less probable than the other, in the same proportion as the comets have less resemblance to this earth, than the planets have.

107. There are many subjects, both speculative and practical, about which analogy is

---

* Essays on Intellectual Powers, essay i. ch. 4.

ANALOGY. 87

the only evidence we can employ. When a lawyer is perplexed with a case, that falls not fairly within the provisions of any existing statute, and for which his file affords no exact precedent, he is placed under the necessity of tracing remote analogies and correspondences between this case and others within his knowledge, and of forming his method of procedure by the equivocal evidence, furnished by such an investigation. To reason correctly on subjects of this nature often requires more caution and discrimination, than are usually required in reasoning on the evidence of testimony or experience. "It is by the urging of different "analogies, that the contention of the bar is "carried on; and it is in the comparison, "adjustment, and reconciliation of them with "one another, that the sagacity and wisdom "of the court are seen and exercised."*

108. Analogy, on account of the uncertainty which attends its conclusions, is rarely employed in scientifick investigations. It serves to guide our judgments, where direct evidence cannot be obtained; and it affords a degree of probability, which is sufficient for the prac-

* Paley, Polit. Phil. ch. 8.

tical business of life. The proper use of this instrument is to defend and illustrate truths, already admitted on other evidence. It assists to explain ambiguities of language, and to exhibit obscure truths in a clear and familiar light.*

CHAPTER FIFTH.

REASONING ON FACTS.

109. A different mode of reasoning from either of the preceding is used in the investigation of those important and interesting truths, which are comprised under the general name of *facts*. These are for the most part so unconnected and independent, so transient in their existence, and so dissimilar in the causes, which produce, and the circumstances, which attend them, that they cannot be deduced from any general principles of reasoning. The proofs, by which alone they can be established, must be derived from impressions, made on the senses

* Locke, Essay on the Understanding, b. iv. ch. 16. Campbell, Phil. Rhet. vol. i. b. i. ch. 5, sect. 2. Beattie, Essay on Truth, part i. ch. 2, sect. 7. Tatham, Chart and Scale of Truth, vol. i. ch. 1 sect. 3. Stewart, Elem. Phil. Mind, vol ii. ch. 4, sect. 4. Gambier, Moral Evidence, ch. 2.

of some persons, to whose immediate observation the facts themselves, or some appearances, connected with them, must have been presented. The truths, belonging to this class, form the largest and most valuable part of our knowledge. They enter into the business of human life; and deeply involve the happiness both of individuals and of communities.

110. Facts may be distinguished into three classes, in reference to the evidence, by which they are judged. Some are admitted on testimony alone; some on circumstantial evidence alone; and some on these two united.

First, human testimony is the evidence, on which we place most reliance for our knowledge of such facts as have not fallen under our immediate observation. We readily admit the reality of a fact on the sober declaration of a person, whose veracity we have no positive reason for distrusting. Truth is naturally agreeable to the human mind; for people usually speak as they think. No effort of invention is required to relate things as they are; but arts of deception require study; and are seldom practised, but for criminal purposes. The moral sense is rarely, if ever, depraved to such a degree, as to lose all preference of truth to falsehood.

111. A propensity to believe what others assert has also its foundation in the constitution of the mind, in the same manner as the tendency to veracity. Children at first believe every thing that is told them; which is a wise provision, as testimony is to them the principal means of obtaining knowledge. This disposition to unlimited credulity continues, till experience begets distrust, and at length teaches the necessity of restraining our confidence in testimony within certain limits.

112. Testimony is either *oral* or *written*. Oral testimony is distinguished into *original*, and *transmitted* or *traditional*. It is *original* when it *is derived from one, who had sensible evidence of the fact asserted*. This is the only testimony of this kind, in which we can have full confidence; and, when accompanied by circumstances of the most favourable nature, produces a firm belief; even though it be the declaration of a single witness.

113. When several independent original witnesses, with equal advantages for knowing the fact, which they assert, and without any

previous concert, agree in their report, they mutually strengthen each other's testimony. This concurrence of several independent testimonies is itself a probability, distinct from that, which may be termed the sum of the probabilities, resulting from the separate testimonies of the witnesses; a probability, which would remain, even though the witnesses were of such a character as to merit no confidence. That such a concurrence should be accidental is in the highest degree improbable. If, therefore, concert be excluded, there remains no other cause for the concurrence, than the existence of the fact.

114. That evidence, which is professedly given on a certain subject, is called *direct testimony*. But a declaration, uttered in familiar conversation, or casually made in the course of a speech or discourse, may be applied as evidence on a subject in no way connected with that, on which it was originally introduced. This is termed *incidental* testimony, and it is usually considered of greater validity than that, which is direct; because, from the manner in which it was introduced, there is less reason

to apprehend any deliberate intention to deceive.

115. When a witness asserts a fact, which he did not personally observe, but which he received from the mouth of some other person, his testimony is called *transmitted* or *traditional*. The general principle with regard to this sort of testimony is, that the further it travels from its original source, that is, from the immediate witness of the fact, the weaker it becomes. The existence of a fact, reported by several persons in succession, becomes a probability, resulting from a series of probabilities, successively founded on each other. Each person can affirm no more than what he received from his immediate informant, and the channel, through which the report was said to have passed from the original witness to him.

116. The circumstances, constituting what is called the *credibility* of a witness, are the following: First, *sufficient discernment, opportunity*, and *attention*, to obtain a clear knowledge of the fact attested. Secondly, *disinterestedness*, which, in its full extent, implies the absence of all expectation of advantage or detriment, arising from the testimony, either to the witness

himself, or to his friends, sect, or party. Thirdly, *integrity*. This affords the strongest assurance of a true testimony, inasmuch as it is absolutely inconsistent with any intention to deceive or prevaricate, as well as with a conscious ignorance of the fact attested. To these may be added the sanction of an oath, with a knowledge of its nature and of the high penalties annexed to perjury. But testimony under oath is principally confined to juridical proceedings. It is rarely employed in settling historical facts, or the ordinary events of human life. So far as a witness is deficient in either of the above qualifications, so far will this deficiency invalidate his testimony.

117. Written testimony is usually esteemed stronger, and more deserving of confidence, than oral; for the record, being made, for the most part, without a knowledge of the uses, to which it is afterwards applied, may be presumed to have been made without any undue bias: and the witness has more time to contemplate the fact, and weigh the circumstances, so as to render his account accurate. Further, as the record of facts is usually made soon after they occur, this testimony is secure against any

suspicions, arising from the imperfection of memory, which often weakens the force of oral testimony, especially on subjects of a distant date, where circumstances are liable to be forgotten, and conjectures substituted in their stead.

118. Written testimony is also less liable to have its credibility impaired by transmission than oral. For, as the original record is commonly preserved for many years, it may be compared with the successive copies, and the slightest disagreement may easily be detected. Whereas oral testimony is fugitive in its nature, and the existence of the original witness must be determined by the testimony of a second witness, whose existence must be admitted, in like manner, on the credibility of a third, and so on. Besides, the care, which copying requires, gives a copy a preference to transmitted oral testimony. Mistake, in the former, is much less likely to be committed.

119. If several independent copies be taken of an original record, and these agree in all material circumstances, their credibility, with respect to the object testified, is nearly equal to that of the original record. For it is highly

probable, that the different copies would substantially agree; and scarcely possible, that the same error should be committed in all. The same remark is applicable to all the successive copies, and the more numerous they are, the more they strengthen each other.

120. In all plural testimony, whether oral or written, the several witnesses are required to agree in every *important* circumstance. But in things of minor consequence, a certain degree of discrepancy tends rather to increase, than to diminish, the credibility of the testimony; for such a discrepancy is what must naturally be expected from different persons, describing the same things.

121. *General notoriety* is a ground of belief, extending both to specifick facts and general truths. It is a species of testimony different from either of the preceding in this, that the information is not derived, *immediately* or *remotely*, from any one, who pretends to have personally witnessed the fact, or investigated the truth in question. No person can examine every subject for himself, so as to have full knowledge of the truth of every proposition, which he finds it necessary to believe. Many

things must be received on trust. Most men can give no better reason for their belief of the greater part of the facts and general truths, which they receive, than that they find them universally believed by others.

122. The weight of this evidence depends partly on the presumption, that, unless the assertions were true, their falsehood would have been detected; and partly on experience; for, though we are in the constant practice of admitting them as unquestionable truths, we rarely find ourselves deceived.

123. This species of evidence should not be applied without discrimination. Mathematical subjects admit of being certainly known, and mistakes respecting them may be easily corrected. In these, therefore, propositions universally believed may be relied on with safety. The same may be observed of all assertions concerning the existence and qualities of material things; and also concerning those facts and events, which are subject to the observation of many persons. But the case is different with respect to those propositions, which, if false, could not be easily disproved; such, for example, as relate to events, which could

have been observed only by a few persons; or to things, supposed to have happened in remote antiquity, or in fabulous ages. *General notoriety* or *universal belief*, with regard to such propositions, is not a sufficient ground of assent.

124. Secondly, there are many events and occurrences, which, as they happen not within the notice of any one, can be judged of only by *a train of circumstances;* and this evidence often produces a higher degree of assurance, than the testimony of living witnesses. Circumstances can neither falsify nor withhold the truth; and an event is considered as well established, when a number of these are of such a nature, that they cannot be satisfactorily accounted for in any way, but by admitting the event in question.

125. Belief, grounded on circumstantial evidence, is usually denominated *presumption;* and presumptions are either *slight* or *violent,* according as the circumstances noticed are more or less necessary to the fact supposed, or do more or less usually and exclusively attend it. Thus, the presumption, that a person is the author of an essay, barely because the hand-

writing resembles his, is only slight; for one person may imitate the hand of another, and two persons may resemble each other in their usual manner of writing. But, to render the presumption violent, the circumstance must be such, not only as would necessarily have attended the fact, had it existed, but such as could not be supposed to have existed; unless the fact in contemplation had existed likewise. Thus, a cottage, discovered on a desolate island, affords a violent presumption, that some human being had been there before. A shelter of some kind would be a natural, if not a necessary consequence of a person's having resided there; and there is no other way, by which the existence of the cottage can be accounted for.

The fact, on which a presumption is grounded, must be clearly proved; for a presumption cannot be raised on a mere conjecture.

126. Thirdly, the credibility of attested facts may be heightened by the *analogy* of those facts *to our general experience in similar cases*, or to what reason would lead us to expect. This analogy is denominated *internal evidence*. Facts, which are rendered probable by inter-

nal evidence, may have their probability increased by testimony, though in different degrees. If an asserted fact agree with our constant and invariable experience, its probability can be but little augmented by the most unexceptionable testimony. Thus, the freezing of water is so common in our climate, that, should any person affirm, that Charles river was frozen over in February, fifty years ago, we could have no hesitancy in believing it. Nor would our assurance of the fact be increased, by the united testimony of five hundred witnesses, of the most undoubted veracity.

127. Where the internal probability is less, more testimony is required to produce belief; as, if it were asserted, that there was thunder in May, or frost in October, in any particular year. These events, happening not uniformly, though much oftener than they fail, receive but a slight confirmation from past experience.

128. Those facts, which are called *indifferent* or *equicasual*, by reason of the irregularity of their appearance, belong exclusively to the province of testimony; as, whether a ship sailed on Tuesday or on Friday; whether a man made his will, or died intestate. The probability

that any asserted fact of this sort happened at any specified time or place, will be just equal to the credibility of the witnesses attesting it.

129. If the asserted fact be of an *extraordinary* nature, and one, that militates with our general experience in similar cases, it will be assented to with difficulty; as, if it were asserted, that there was snow in August, or that the same number drew the highest prize in five successive lotteries. The internal improbability of such facts must be overcome by an increased weight of testimony.

130. Those facts or events, which are admitted with the greatest difficulty of all, are such as are *supernatural*, or *miraculous*. These, contradicting our invariable experience, and opposing the well known laws of corporeal nature, are in themselves in the highest degree improbable; and require for their belief a testimony so ample, and attended by such circumstances, as would render its falsehood no les miraculous than the fact attested.*

* Gilbert, Law of Evidence. Kirwan, Logick, part iii. ch. 6. Locke, Essay on the Understanding, b. iv. ch. 16. Gambier, Moral Evidence, ch. 2.

CHAPTER SIXTH.

CALCULATION OF CHANCES.

131. By *chance* is not meant the negation of a cause, but our ignorance of it. Every change in the universe must proceed from some adequate cause. When we speak of events as happening *fortuitously*, or by *chance*, we mean no more, than that the causes, which produce them, are wholly unknown to us. The bare possibility of an event is often denominated a chance; and where there are several known causes equally capable of producing different events, it is manifest, that there are so many chances of those events; and that no one of them is more probable than the rest.

132. The *doctrine of chances is that, which teaches the degree of probability or improbability of any one of a given number of events, considered as equally possible.* Thus, on throwing a die, it is certain that some one of its six faces will be turned up; but, as only one of these six faces can present an ace, the chance of throwing an ace is only one out of six chances, or $\frac{1}{6}$; and the chances against it are five out of six, or $\frac{5}{6}$ of a certainty. Hence the general rule

is, that *the probability or improbability of any event is, as the number of the favourable chances, divided by the sum of all the chances, both favourable and unfavourable.*

133. The degree of probability, that any event will or will not happen, is conveniently expressed by a fraction, whose numerator represents the number of chances, which favour the existence, or the nonexistence of the event; and whose denominator is the sum of all the chances, both favourable and adverse to the event. Thus, if an event have five chances to happen and three to fail, the fraction $\frac{5}{8}$ will express the probability of its happening, and the fraction $\frac{3}{8}$, that of its failure. These two fractions, which represent all the chances, both of happening and failing, being added together, their sum will always be equal to unity; since the sum of their numerators will be just equal to their common denominator. And as in every case it is certain, that an event will either happen or fail, it follows, that certainty is justly represented by unity.

134. The expectation of obtaining a benefit which depends on the happening of an uncertain event, has a determinate value before the

CALCULATION OF CHANCES. 103

event takes place. The value of this expectation is in all cases estimated by multiplying the value of the benefit expected by the fraction, which represents the probability of obtaining it. Thus, if 60 crowns be promised a person on condition of his throwing a particular face on a die, his expectation before trial is worth 10 crowns, since he has one chance in six, or $\frac{1}{6}$ of a certainty of gaining the whole sum.

135. Events are either *independent* or *dependent*. *Two events are independent, when they have no connexion with each other, and the happening of one neither promotes nor hinders the happening of the other*. Thus, throwing an ace on one die affects not the possibility of throwing it again on the same, or on another die. But the possibility of a *joint event* on two dice, though each is independent of the other, singly considered, is affected by all the possibilities of failure in each of the conjoined events. Now there are thirty-six possible events on two dice considered conjointly; for each has six faces, and each face of the one may be combined with each face of the other. Therefore the possible appearances are $6 \times 6 = 36$. But, of these combinations, there is but one pro-

ductive of the appearance of two aces, or any other two faces. So that the chance of throwing two aces either together on two dice, or successively on one die, is only $\frac{1}{36}$.

136. Hence the probability of two or more independent but joint events is equal to the product of the chances of each. Thus, the probability of throwing three aces successively on one die is $\frac{1}{6} \times \frac{1}{6} \times \frac{1}{6} = \frac{1}{216}$. So if the probability, that one man, A, will live a year, be $\frac{9}{10}$, and the probability of the life of another man, B, for one year, be $\frac{9}{10}$, the probability, that both will live another year, is but $\frac{9}{10} \times \frac{9}{10} = \frac{81}{100}$. Hence the concurrence of two events is less probable than the occurrence of either; and is even improbable, though each is probable and completely independent of the other.

137. From the foregoing rule it is manifest, that the joint occurrence of two or more equi-casual, independent events is improbable; and the more so, the more numerous they are. For the probability of each is $\frac{1}{2}$; therefore the joint chance of two such events is $\frac{1}{2} \times \frac{1}{2} = \frac{1}{4}$; and of three such events is $\frac{1}{2} \times \frac{1}{2} \times \frac{1}{2} = \frac{1}{8}$. So the concurrence of two independent, improbable facts is still more improbable. For, supposing the

CALCULATION OF CHANCES. 105

improbability of one of them to be $\frac{1}{4}$, and that of the other $\frac{1}{5}$, their joint improbability would be $\frac{1}{20}$. By the same rule, the improbability of the death of A within a year being $\frac{4}{10}$, and that of the death of B within a year $\frac{2}{10}$, the improbability, that both will die within a year, is $\frac{4}{10} \times \frac{2}{10} = \frac{8}{100}$. And the probability that one of the events will happen and the other fail is, as the probability of the happening of the one, multiplied by the probability of the failure of the other. So, in the above case, the probability, that A will live and that B will die, is $\frac{6}{10} \times \frac{2}{10} = \frac{12}{100}$. And the probability, that B will live and that A will die, is $\frac{8}{10} \times \frac{4}{10} = \frac{32}{100}$.

138. *A dependent event is one, whose existence is rendered more or less probable by the chances attending the existence of another event.* When several events are connected in such a manner, that the second depends on the first, the third on the second, and so on, the probability of the first or independent event must be first ascertained; that of the second, which depends on the first, is then found, by multiplying its separate probability into that of the first; and the product will give the real

106 CALCULATION OF CHANCES.

probability of the second event. In the same manner we proceed to find the probability of a third or fourth dependent event.

139. Thus, suppose six white and six black balls to be placed in a box, and through a hole in the box, two balls to be successively drawn out; and let it be required to determine the probability, that both these will be white. As there are twelve balls in the box, and six of them are white, it is evident, that the probability of drawing a white ball at the first trial will be $\frac{6}{12}$. But the chance of doing this on the second trial will be different; for, as one of the balls has been taken out, there are but eleven remaining; and since, in order to the second trial, it is necessary to suppose, that the ball removed was a white one, the remaining number of these is reduced to five. The separate probability, therefore, of drawing a white ball at the second trial will be only $\frac{5}{11}$; and the chance of drawing it the first and second time will be $\frac{6}{12} = \frac{1}{2} \times \frac{5}{11} = \frac{5}{22}$. The separate probability of drawing out a white ball at a third trial, since two white balls have been removed, will be $\frac{4}{10}$; and the chance of drawing three white ones at three successive trials will be $\frac{1}{2} \times \frac{5}{11} \times \frac{4}{10} = \frac{10}{220} = \frac{1}{11}$.

140. Again, W sailed for Africa in a fleet of twelve ships, three of which were lost in a storm, on the first part of the voyage. Of the crews of the nine ships, that escaped the storm, one third part perished from the hardships, they met on the voyage. We wish to ascertain the probability, that W has escaped both calamities. Now, as the chance of his having survived the hardships of the voyage depends on the event of his having escaped the storm, the probability of the last named event must be first ascertained. If this be found improbable, the second event must fail; but if it be found probable, the second event may exist, and the probability of its existence may be found by the rule already given. [No. 138.]

141. As nine ships out of the twelve survived the storm, the probability that W escaped in one of them is $\frac{9}{12} = \frac{3}{4}$. This being supposed, the probability of his having escaped the second danger, since only one third of those, who survived the storm, perished, is $\frac{2}{3}$. Hence the probability of his having lived through both dangers is $\frac{3}{4} \times \frac{2}{3} = \frac{6}{12} = \frac{1}{2}$. Therefore it is merely doubtful whether he survived both calamities. If only $\frac{1}{4}$ of the crew survived the

108　DEMONSTRATIVE REASONING.

second danger, then his escape would be improbable; for $\frac{1}{6} \times \frac{1}{2} = \frac{1}{12}$. If only two out of the twelve ships were lost, and consequently ten had escaped the first danger, and $\frac{2}{3}$ of the crew had escaped the second danger, as above, then the probability of his entire survival would be $\frac{10}{12} \times \frac{2}{3} = \frac{20}{36} = \frac{5}{9}$; a slight probability.*

CHAPTER SEVENTH.

GENERAL DESCRIPTION OF DEMONSTRATIVE REASONING.

142. The general nature of *demonstrative reasoning* has already been explained, in pointing out the circumstances, which distinguish it from moral, or probable reasoning. [See No 87 to 93.] It has generally been admitted, that demonstration can be employed only about such truths as have been termed *necessary*, the subjects of which are not supposed to have any real existence, but to be abstractly conceived by the mind. All created beings depend on the will of their Creator. Their existence, their properties, and of course the relations, subsisting among those properties, are contin-

* Demoivre, Doctrine of Chances, Introduction. Kirwan, Logick part iii. ch. 7.

gent, and perpetually varying. Our reasoning on these must be grounded on the observation of our senses; and the conclusions, which we make, are liable to be uncertain. But demonstrative reasoning, being grounded on exact and adequate definitions, and proceeding by the successive application of general propositions, which have an intuitive agreement with each other, affords satisfaction in every step; and the mind advances to the conclusion with the fullest assurance of certainty.

143. Demonstration is best adapted to the exact sciences of number and quantity. Arithmetick and geometry possess many important advantages with respect to this method of reasoning. Their terms are free from all ambiguity. Their first principles are simple and obvious. The subjects, about which they are conversant, are wholly independent of things in actual existence, and capable of being perfectly defined. The properties belonging to these subjects, and their various relations, are necessary and immutable. These circumstances impart to mathematical demonstrations a clearness and force, which cannot be obtained

110 DEMONSTRATIVE REASONING.

in other sciences. For these reasons many have maintained, that demonstrative reasoning can be used *only* within the precincts of mathematicks. Many others have controverted this position; and have contended, that this method may, at least occasionally, be employed in other sciences.

144. Mr. Locke advanced the opinion, that moral subjects are as susceptible of demonstration as mathematical. His reason for this opinion is thus stated in his Essay on the Understanding:* " The precise, real essence " of the things, moral words stand for, may " be perfectly known; and so the congruity or " incongruity of the things themselves be cer- ' tainly discovered; in which consists perfect "knowledge." He adds, "*definition* is the " only way whereby the precise meaning of " moral words can be known; and yet a way, " whereby their meaning may be known *cer-* " *tainly*, and without leaving any room for " contest." In another place† he says, "the " relation of other modes may certainly be " perceived, as well as those of number and

* Book iii. ch. 11, sect 16.
† Book iv. ch. 3, sect. 18.

"extension; and I cannot see why they should
"not also be capable of demonstration, if due
"methods were thought on to examine or pur-
"sue their agreement or disagreement."

145. Dr. Reid distinguishes demonstrative reasoning into two kinds, which are metaphysical and mathematical. "In metaphysical "reasoning," he observes, "the process is "always short. The conclusion is but a step "or two, seldom more, from the first principle "or axiom, on which it is grounded; and the "different conclusions depend not one upon "another. It is otherwise in mathematical "reasoning. Here the field has no limits. One "proposition leads to another; that to a third, "and so on without end. If it should be asked, "why demonstrative reasoning has so wide "a field in mathematicks, while, in other "abstract subjects, it is confined within very "narrow limits; I conceive this chiefly owing "to the nature of quantity, the object of math-"ematicks."*

146. Demonstration, in the customary sense of the term, appears not to be absolutely circumscribed by the narrow limits of a single

---

* Essays on the Intellectual Powers, essay vii. ch. 1.

science. Wherever the subjects of our reasoning are independent on the existence of things, and are of a nature to afford exact definitions and general propositions of undoubted certainty, there this method of reasoning may be employed. And it appears unnecessary to concede, that these elements of demonstration are no where to be found, except in the science of mathematicks.

147. Professor Scott, speaking of Dr. Reid's division of demonstrative reasoning, says; " It "evidently cannot be meant by Dr. Reid, that "metaphysicks is a science demonstrable in all "its parts, like mathematicks. He was too " well acquainted with the general uncertainty " of metaphysical speculations to have advanc- "ed such an opinion. If then he asserts only, "that several metaphysical truths admit of "demonstration, the same ought doubtless to "be said of physicks, many of the reasonings "of which have at least as much of demonstra- "tive certainty as any of the speculations of "metaphysicks. The truth appears to be "that every branch of science may occasional "ly assume the demonstrative form. The ex- "istence of a Deity, the immateriality of the

"human soul, and other moral or metaphysical
"truths, have perhaps been as fairly demon-
"strated as the Pythagorean proposition, or
"the parabolick motion of projectiles. But
"some sciences are much more susceptible of
"this kind of proof then others; physicks
"admitting much more of demonstration than
"metaphysicks, or morals. Of all the sciences,
"mathematicks is that, which admits the most
"largely of demonstration. Its first principles
"are so certain, so definite, and clear; and its
"manner of proof so accurate and legitimate,
"that it may fairly be called a completely de-
"monstrative science, and the only one, which
"is justly entitled to that name."*

CHAPTER EIGHTH.

DISTINCTIONS OF REASONING.

148. Reasoning is further distinguished into that, which is *a priori*, and that, which is *a posteriori*. *Reasoning* a priori *is that, which deduces consequences from definitions formed, or principles assumed; or which infers effects from causes previously known.* The books of

* Elem. of Intell. Phil. chap. 8, sect. 4.

mathematicks afford numerous instances of conclusions legitimately drawn from definitions and assumed principles. We also reason *a priori* whenever we judge of effects from a knowledge of the causes, which produce them. Thus we infer, that an eclipse of the sun and an eclipse of the moon can never happen within twelve days of each other, from our knowledge of the causes, which occasion those phenomena.

149. Reasoning *a posteriori* is the reverse of the former process. By this we deduce causes from effects. Thus, we infer that the earth is spherical from its shadow on the moon in a lunar eclipse; and we infer the being of a God from our own existence and that of the objects around us. All reasoning concerning the properties and laws, both of mind and body, proceeds on this principle. It is only by a careful observation of facts, that the laws, which regulate them, can be discovered.

150. Another distinction of reasoning is into *direct* and *indirect*. *The reasoning is direct, when the proofs are so applied, as to show immediately the agreement or repugnancy between the subject and predicate of the proposition*

in question. In indirect reasoning, the arguments, which we employ, are not intended *primarily* to show the relation between the term of the proposition, whose truth we would establish; but to prove the falsehood or absurdity of the proposition, to which it is opposed. This method may be adopted, whenever it is manifest, that the proposition, which we allege, or its contrary, must be true. We may then prove the impossibility of the contrary proposition; or we may show, that a manifest absurdity must follow from admitting it; and in either case we establish the truth of our original proposition. The former course is usually called a proof *per impossibile*; and the latter, a *reductio ad absurdum*.

151. Mathematicians make frequent use of indirect reasoning. Thus, Euclid proves, by an indirect course, that, "if two circles touch "each other internally, they cannot have the "same centre." He first supposes the contrary to be true, namely, that the two circles have the same centre; and no third supposition can be made; for they must either both have the same centre or not. He then demonstrates the impossibility of the case assumed; and thence

116 SYLLOGISTICK REASONING.

infers the truth of the proposition, which he first asserted. So moralists prove the existence of an all-wise and powerful Creator, by tracing the absurdities, which the contrary supposition involves.

152. Another form of indirect reasoning, in frequent use, is denominated reasoning *a fortiori*. This consists in deducing a proposition, as true, from less obvious propositions, embraced by the same general principles. Thus, if the felon, who robs on the highway, deserves the punishment of death, this retribution is due *a fortiori* to the wretch, who has committed parricide.

CHAPTER NINTH.

GENERAL DESCRIPTION OF SYLLOGISTICK REASONING.

153. All reasoning proceeds by comparison; and two comparisons are necessary to enable us to make a conclusion. The subject and predicate of the proposition to be proved must be separately compared with some third term, or common measure; and from these comparisons we infer their agreement or repugnancy.

This process, when expressed in words, consists of three propositions, and has been termed *syllogism.**

154. Syllogism was regarded, for many centuries, as the only sure instrument of reasoning; and skill in the use of it as the highest accomplishment, which the mind can possess. It derived its celebrity from the talents and industry of Aristotle, who traced and analyzed its principles, subjected it to laws, and exhibited it in all the variety of *modes* and *figures*, into which it could be moulded. Since the time of that philosopher, the name *syllogism* has usually been employed to denote an argument, framed according to certain technical rules of art. But it is sometimes used in a larger sense, to imply any process of reasoning from more general to less general, in opposition to the principle of analytical induction. In this sense, it will apply to mathematical reasoning; for all demonstrations in this science proceed on this fundamental principle of the syllogism, that *whatever may be affirmed of any genus may be affirmed of all the species included under it.*

* Συλλογισμός, *computatio*, a συλλογίζομαι, *colligo*, *ratiocinor*, *computo*.

155. Syllogism and induction proceed in opposite directions. Induction, as has already been observed, begins with individual objects, as they exist in nature, and ascends by successive steps to the most general truths. Syllogism begins where induction terminates. It commences with some universal proposition, and follows back the footsteps of the former process, transferring at each stage the predicate of the more general to the less general rank of beings; or, in other words, predicating the genus of the species, and the species of the individual.

156. The difference of these methods may be shown by the following example. We observe that the individual people of our acquaintance are constantly dying around us; that men rarely live to the age of a hundred years, and that the former generations are wholly swept from the earth. From these facts we infer, that death is the common lot of our species. Observing also, that the same fatality attends the various species of beasts, birds, and insects, we deduce the more general conclusion, that *all animals are mortal*. This inductive process, reversed in syllogistick language, would run thus,

SYLLOGISTICK REASONING. 119

All animals are mortal;
All men are animals;
Therefore all men are mortal;

All men are mortal.
W. X. Y. are men;
Therefore W. X. Y. are mortal.

157. Syllogism is employed with advantage in communicating to others, in an exact and perspicuous manner, the general principles of science. It may also be used with success in exposing the weakness of arguments, stated in loose or figurative language. But it is of no service in helping us to the discovery of new truths. We must know a thing first, Mr. Locke observes,* and then we can prove it syllogistically.

158. As syllogism operates wholly on general propositions, and definitions previously established, the justness of its conclusions must depend ultimately on the accuracy, with which the inductive processes have been conducted. "The syllogism," says Lord Bacon, "is form-"ed of propositions; propositions, of words "and words are the marks of ideas. If there-"fore ideas themselves, which make the ground-"work of our reasonings, are confused, and

* Essay, b. iv. ch. 17.

"formed from a hasty observation of things, the conclusions, which we make from them, will be without solidity. The whole therefore depends on the accuracy of our inductions."*

CHAPTER TENTH.
OF REGULAR SYLLOGISMS.

159. The most general division of syllogisms is into *single* and *compound*. Of single syllogisms, some are *regular* and some are *irregular*. *A regular syllogism is an argument, consisting of three propositions, the last of which is deduced from the two preceding, and is substantially contained in them.* Example:

Every human virtue should be habitually practised;
Industry and temperance are human virtues;
Therefore industry and temperance should be habitually practised.

160. This is a concise and luminous method of evincing the agreement or repugnancy between the subject and predicate of a proposi-

---

* "Syllogismus ex propositionibus constat; propositiones, ex "verbis; verba notionum tesseræ sunt. Itaque si notiones ipsæ, "id quod basis rei est, confusæ sint, et temerè a rebus abstractæ "nihil in iis, quæ superstruuntur, est firmitudinis. Itaque spes est "una in inductione vera. *Novum Organum,* lib. i. aph. 14.

REGULAR SYLLOGISMS. 121

tion. A third term, having a common relation to them both, is invented, and applied to them successively, in two distinct propositions. These are called *premises*, because from them the proposed question is inferred, as a conclusion; and its subject and predicate are either joined or separated, according as they were found in the premises to agree, or not, with the term introduced. It is obvious, that, *if any two things agree with a third, they must agree with each other;* and that *two things, of which one agrees, and the other disagrees with a third, must disagree with each other.* The former of these rules is the foundation of all affirmative conclusions, and the latter of all negative.

161. The names of the three propositions are the *major*, the *minor*, and the *conclusion*. These are composed of three terms, denominated the *major*, the *minor*, and the *middle terms. The predicate of the conclusion is called the major term,** because it is the most general; and *the subject of the conclusion the minor term*, because it is the least general. These two are also denominated the *extremes;* and the *third*

---
* See note B, at the end of the book.

term, introduced as a common measure between them, is called the *mean* or *middle term*, because its extension is less than that of the major, and greater than that of the minor term. [See No. 35.] This circumstance proves the natural situation of the middle term to be that of subject in the major premise, and of predicate in the minor; since the predicate of a proposition is never less, but usually more general, than the subject.

162. In forming the syllogism, each term is taken twice, and no more. *The middle and major terms constitute the major premise; the minor and middle terms the minor premise; and the two extremes, connected by a copula, make up the conclusion.* The major proposition must always be universal, but may be either affirmative or negative; and the minor proposition must always be affirmative, but may be either universal or particular.* The conclusion may be either universal affirmative universal negative, particular affirmative, or particular negative.

163. In every regular syllogism, the major proposition is placed first; the minor next.

---

* See note C, at the end of the book.

and the conclusion last; as in the following example.

> Every vegetable is combustible;
> Every tree is a vegetable;
> Therefore every tree is combustible.

Combustible is the major term; *every tree* the minor term; and these extremes are joined in the conclusion. *Vegetable* is the middle term; it is subjected in the major premise, and predicated in the minor. The major premise must always be sufficiently general to involve the conclusion; and must be assumed as a truth already known. It cannot be proved by syllogism. This instrument teaches only how to make a legitimate inference of one proposition from another.

164. The truth, proved by the preceding example, is, that trees are combustible. The major premise, namely, every vegetable is combustible, is first assumed on the ground of experience and observation. The minor premise barely asserts the fact, that trees belong to the class of vegetables. Now if it be certain, that combustion belongs universally to vegetables, and that trees are included in that class of things, it must of necessity follow, that every

tree is combustible; for it is a primary law of syllogistick reasoning, that *whatever may be affirmed of any general term, may be affirmed of every species and individual included within its extension.*

165. In the regular syllogism, each step of the reasoning process is distinctly expressed; but, in familiar language, one part is frequently omitted, which may be readily found by examining the grounds, on which the judgment is formed. Thus,

> No language is perfect;
> Because it is a human invention.

Perfection is here denied of language, for no other assigned reason, than because it is a human invention. But there is a latent proposition, which is the real ground of the judgment, and must therefore have been distinctly contemplated by the mind, namely, *no human invention is perfect.* Let this proposition be subjoined to the other two, and the argument will stand thus;

> No language is perfect;
> Because it is a human invention;
> And no human invention is perfect.

This is the regular syllogism reversed; which, rectified, will stand thus;

> No human invention is perfect;
> Every language is a human invention;
> Therefore no language is perfect.

166. Every assertion, accompanied by a reason why it is made, contains the elements of a syllogism, namely, the major, minor, and middle terms. Every such assertion made in the familiar form of language, may be transferred to a regular syllogism, by observing the following rule: First, distinguish the reason, on which the attribute of the given proposition is affirmed or denied of its subject, and this will be the middle term of the syllogism. Let this be taken, in its most enlarged sense, for the subject of a proposition, to which, for a predicate, unite the attribute of the asserted proposition, and the major premise will be formed. Next, to form the minor premise, we have only to predicate the middle term, already found, of the subject of the asserted proposition. The original proposition, without the reason, before annexed to it, will constitute the conclusion of the syllogism.

167. For example, Dr. Johnson says of envy, "It is, above all other vices, inconsistent "with the character of a social being, *because*

"it sacrifices truth and kindness to very weak "temptations." *Sacrifices truth and kindness to very weak temptations* is the reason, why envy is pronounced, above all other vices, inconsistent with the character of a social being. This, then, must form the middle term of the syllogism. But as this collection of words represents an attribute, and not a person or thing really existing, it cannot be enlarged, so as to become the subject of a general proposition, by simply placing before it one of the common signs of universality, *all, every*, or *each;* it must be preceded by some universal sign of a different sort, as *whatever, that, which,* or the like. Thus;

That which sacrifices truth and kindness to very weak temptations is, above all other vices, inconsistent with the character of a social being;

Envy sacrifices truth and kindness to very weak temptations;

Therefore *envy* is, above all other vices, inconsistent with the character of a social being.

In this manner may the simple elements of reasoning, however obscured, in any instance, by rhetorical language, or complicated forms of speech, be easily collected, and exhibited in a regular syllogism.

168. As the major proposition of a syllogism must always be universal, the middle term, as the subject of this proposition, must be taken in a universal sense. Every middle term must represent either some class of persons or things, or else some attribute common to a whole class of beings. If the middle term denote persons or things, something must be asserted, hypothetically, in the major proposition, to agree with, or to be repugnant to, that whole class of beings; and in this class the minor term must be included; which it is the sole business of the minor proposition to affirm. In the conclusion, we apply to the minor term, separately, the same predicate, which was applied to it in the major proposition, in connexion with the whole class of things, to which it belongs.

169. If the middle term express an attribute, it must be asserted in the major proposition, that, to whatever person or thing the attribute, forming the middle term, can be ascribed, the major term may be ascribed also. In the minor proposition, the attribute, which forms the middle term, is declared applicable to the minor term. In the conclusion, the agreement or repugnancy, which was before

admitted between the middle and major terms, must be also admitted between the major and minor terms.

170. Any regular syllogism may be reduced to the familiar form of reasoning by the following rule: First, state the conclusion, omitting the illative *therefore;* then, subjoin the middle term together with the minor, or some pronoun as its substitute, preceded by some causal particle, as *since, for*, or *because*. For example,

Every animal, possessing wings and feathers, is a bird;
An ostrich is an animal, possessing wings and feathers,
Therefore an ostrich is a bird.

This syllogism may be thus expressed in the familiar form of reasoning;

An ostrich is a bird;
Because it has wings and feathers.

171. Each of the preceding syllogisms concludes with a universal proposition. The conclusions of the four following examples are of different kinds.

I.

Whoever disregards the rights of his fellow beings, deserves the detestation of mankind;
Tyrants disregard the rights of their fellow beings;
Therefore tyrants deserve the detestation of mankind.

II.

They, who subvert the foundations of morality and religion, ought not to be respected;
Atheists subvert the foundations of morality and religion;
Therefore atheists ought not to be respected.

III.

Every creature, which can live in more elements than one, is amphibious;
Some animals can live in more elements than one;
Therefore some animals are amphibious.

IV.

No person of dissolute habits can be a safe companion;
Some persons of improved minds are dissolute in their habits;
Therefore some persons of improved minds are not safe companions.

The conclusion of the first syllogism is a universal affirmative proposition; that of the second, a universal negative; that of the third, a particular affirmative; and that of the fourth, a particular negative. These are all the kinds, into which propositions are distinguished, in reference to quantity and quality.[*]

---

[*] Common systems of Logick. Collard, Logick, part iv. ch. 4, 5

CHAPTER ELEVENTH.

ENTHYMEMES.

172. Besides the regular, categorical syllogism, described in the preceding chapter, there are some other kinds of single syllogisms, which have different degrees of irregularity in their construction. Among these may be placed the *enthymeme*, which is an abridged, or defective syllogism, consisting of the conclusion and only one of the premises; the other being suppressed, as too obvious to need insertion. It is of very general use, both in writing and conversation.

173. Which of the premises is omitted in any instance may be known, by the following rule: *If the subject of the conclusion be expressed in the given premise, or proposition, containing the reason, the major premise is omitted; if the predicate of the conclusion be expressed, the minor premise is wanting.* Thus,

Whatever tends to subvert the civil government should be deprecated;
Therefore civil disssenions should be deprecated.

Christianity teaches the way to future happiness;
Therefore *it* should be diligently sought.

The minor premise is omitted in the first example, and the major in the second. Let these be supplied, and the syllogisms will be complete.

Whatever tends to subvert the civil government should be deprecated;
Civil dissensions tend to subvert the civil government;
Therefore civil dissensions should be deprecated.

That knowledge, which teaches the way to future happiness, should be diligently sought;
Christianity teaches the way to future happiness;
Therefore Christianity should be diligently sought.

174. Enthymemes may be expressed in various ways, and have sometimes been distinguished into several kinds. Those are the most regular, which conform to the syllogistick order. In these the conclusion is placed after the proposition, which contains the proof; and, by supplying the omitted proposition, the syllogism is rendered perfect, without any other alteration. But, in familiar conversation, it is more common to express the conclusion first, and then subjoin the reason, on which it is grounded, preceded by a causal particle. As,

Enthusiasm should be avoided;
Because it leads us astray from reason.

They, who deny a future state of retribution, are in error;
For they deny the doctrine of the Bible.

175. Although the conclusion be placed after the reasoning proposition, still the enthymeme will not be regular, unless the syllogistick language and arrangement be employed. The following sentence is an enthymeme of this sort:

"Since it is the understanding, that sets man above the "rest of sensible beings, and gives him all the ad- "vantage and dominion, which he has over them;
"It is certainly a subject, even for its nobleness, worth "our labour to inquire into."

Each of these enthymemes contains the elements of a syllogism, namely, the major, minor, and middle terms; which may be easily distinguished. The suppressed propositions are readily supplied by the mind; and the omission of them contributes to the brevity and elegance of language.

176. An act of reasoning may be stated hypothetically; thus,

The African slave-trade should be discountenanced;
If it be a violation of the natural rights of man.

* Locke, Essay, Introduction.

Here the predicate, *discountenanced*, is not applied to the African slave-trade *absolutely*; but only on condition of its being a violation of man's natural liberty. Still the reasoning is the same, as if it were expressed in this absolute form:

The African slave-trade is a violation of the natural rights of man;
Therefore *it* should be discountenanced by all.

The judgment is formed in the two cases by a comparison of precisely the same things.

177. What are here considered as familiar enthymemes have usually been received as compound propositions, and have been distributed into different species under the heads of *causal, discretive,* and *conditional*. But, that they cannot justly be regarded as mere propositions of any sort, is evident from this, that each example contains two entire propositions. [See No. 80.] It is equally manifest, that they represent complete acts of reasoning, since in each the elements of a perfect syllogism are expressed.*

* Collard, Logick, part iv. ch. 6.

CHAPTER TWELFTH.

CONDITIONAL AND DISJUNCTIVE SYLLOGISMS.

178. *A conditional or hypothetical syllogism is one, whose major proposition is conditional.* Thus,

If men have vicious propensities, they need the restraints of government;
But men have vicious propensities;
Therefore they need the restraints of government.

The major premise consists of two entire propositions, which make an enthymeme. The minor premise and the conclusion constitute another enthymeme, expressing the same meaning as the other, with only this difference, that what is stated hypothetically in the first is expressed absolutely in the last. The first part of the major, containing the condition, is called the *antecedent;* and the last, which contains the conclusion, the *consequent.* If the antecedent be admitted in the minor premise, the consequent must be admitted in the conclusion; for the condition, stated in the antecedent, must always be such as necessarily to require the truth of the consequent. By the same necessity it will follow, that, if the consequent be contradicted in the minor, the antecedent must be contradicted in the conclusion. Thus,

If death be an eternal sleep, the Scriptures are not true;
But the Scriptures are true;
Therefore death is not an eternal sleep.

179. In conditional syllogisms then there are two ways of reasoning, which lead to certain conclusions. The first is called arguing from the position of the antecedent to the position of the consequent; and the other, arguing from the removal of the consequent to the removal of the antecedent. These are the only modes of true reasoning in this sort of syllogism; for we are not at liberty to adopt the contrary course, and argue from the admission of the consequent to the admission of the antecedent, nor from the removal of the antecedent to the removal of the consequent. This will be manifest in the following example:

> If W. were a general, he would have power;
> But W. is not a general;
> Therefore he has not power.

> If W. be a general, he must be obeyed;
> But W. must be obeyed;
> Therefore he is a general.

The falsehood of the consequent will not follow from the falsehood of the antecedent, nor the truth of the antecedent from the truth of the consequent. The one may be true, and the other may be false, for different reasons from those, which are assigned.

180. *A disjunctive syllogism is one, whose major premise is disjunctive.* Thus,

The world is either self-existent, or the work of some finite, or of some infinite Being;
But it is not self-existent, nor the work of any finite being;
Therefore it is the work of an infinite Being.

The business of the major proposition of this syllogism appears to be to enumerate several predicates, of which one only can belong to the subject. If then the minor establishes one of these predicates, the conclusion must remove all the rest; or if, in the minor premise, all the predicates but one are removed, the conclusion must establish that, which remains. This procedure has been denominated arguing from the assertion of one to the rejection of the rest; or, from the denial of one, two, or more, to the establishment of the remainder. But the term *arguing* is applied to it without any good reason, since it is nothing more than a formal and circuitous method of stating a fact.

CHAPTER THIRTEENTH.
COMPOUND SYLLOGISMS.

181. *A compound syllogism consists of more than three propositions, and may be resolved into two or more syllogisms.* Of these the principal kinds are the *Epichirema, Dilemma,* and *Sorites.*

The Epichirema is a compound argument, of which the major and minor premises are separately proved, before the conclusion is drawn. Example.

Unjust laws endanger the stability of government; for they create discontent among the people;

Laws, which restrain the freedom of conscience, are unjust; for they require people to abandon their dearest concerns;

Therefore laws, which restrain the freedom of conscience endanger the stability of government.

The major and minor premises, with their respective proofs, form two enthymemes, which may readily be reduced to regular syllogisms. Discard these proofs, and a regular syllogism will remain.

182. The epichirema is much used in conversation, publick harangues, and oratorical discourses. Cicero's defence of Milo is an argument of this sort. His first position is, that *it is lawful for one man to kill another, who lies in wait to kill him.* This he proves from the laws of nature and the customs of mankind. His second position is, that *Clodius lay in wait for Milo with a murderous intent;* which he proves by his equipage, arms, guards, and other circumstances. Then he infers the conclusion, namely, that *it was lawful for Milo to kill Clodius.*

183. *The Dilemma* is a compound argument, which establishes a general conclusion, either directly by proving its necessity, or indirectly by showing the impossibility or absurdity of its contrary, in every supposable case.* Thus,

Every magistrate must either execute the laws, or suffer them to be violated;
If he execute them, he will be hated by the vicious and profligate:
If he suffer them to be violated, he will be hated by the wise and virtuous;
Therefore, every magistrate is exposed to hatred from his fellow men.

---

* Δις, *bis,* and λαμβάνω, *capio.*

The subject of the conclusion is first divided into two classes, namely, those magistrates, who do, and those who do not execute the laws. The attribute, *hatred*, is then affirmed of each class separately, and is finally predicated of the whole subject. This dilemma may be resolved into three regular syllogisms. The major premise and the conclusion, taken together, constitute a regular enthymeme; and the four intervening propositions form two enthymemes, hypothetically stated.

184. Pyrrho, the ancient sceptick, asserted, that no one can have certain knowledge of any thing. One of his friends reproved him in the following dilemma:

You either know what you say to be true, or you do not know it;

If you do know it to be true, that very knowledge proves your assertion to be false, and you do wrong to make it;

If you do not know it to be true, you do wrong to assert it, since no one has a right to assert what he does not know to be true;

Therefore, in either case, you do wrong to assert, that no one can have certain knowledge of any thing.

185. A dilemma is a form of argument frequently employed both in moral and math-

ematical reasoning. The geometrician adopts this method, when, in order to prove the equality of two lines or angles, he first assumes, that if they are not equal, one must be either greater or less than the other; and, having removed both these suppositions, he thence infers, that the proposed lines or angles are equal.

186. In order to understand fully the principle of reasoning in a dilemma, it is necessary to consider the major premise as conditional, the first part of which is commonly omitted, to wit, the antecedent, which consists of a general assertion, conditionally made, which it is the object of the dilemma to disprove. What usually appears as the major premise, is only the consequent of this number, consisting of an enumeration of all the suppositions, of which the subject will admit.* If then all these suppositions be rejected in the minor premise, the antecedent will of necessity be rejected in the conclusion. This reasoning proceeds univer-

---

* By supplying the antecedent in the example first stated, the major premise will stand thus:

If all magistrates be not exposed to the hatred of their fellow men, it is either because they execute the laws, or suffer them to be violated.

sally from the removal of the consequent to the removal of the antecedent.

187. A dilemma may be defective in two ways; first, when the conditions are not accurately stated in the major premise; secondly, when the argument may be retorted with equal force on him, who offers it. A remarkable instance of the retort of a dilemma happened in the singular controversy between Protagoras and Euathlus. The former engaged to teach the latter the art of pleading for a stipulated reward, one moiety of which was to be paid in hand, and the other when the pupil gained his first cause at court. After a short time Protagoras sued Euathlus for the remaining moiety of the money, and made use of this dilemma:

The case must be decided either in my favour or in yours;
If it is decided in my favour, the sum will be due to me according to the sentence of the judge;
If it is decided in your favour, it will be due to me by virtue of our contract;
Therefore, whether I gain or lose the cause, I shall obtain the reward.

Euathlus thus retorted the dilemma.

I shall either gain the cause, or lose it;
If I gain the cause, nothing will be due to you according to the sentence of the judge;
If I lose the cause, nothing will be due to you according to our contract;
Therefore in neither case shall I pay you the reward.

Sometimes the consequent of the major consists of more than two parts, and then the syllogism is called a *trilemma, tesseralemma*, and so on.

188. *The Sorites* is an irregular, compound argument, consisting of a series of propositions, arranged in such a manner, that the predicate of each preceding proposition forms the subject of that which follows; and the concluding proposition unites its predicate to the subject of the first.* Thus,

Avaricious men have many desires;
They, who have many desires, are in want of many things;
They, who are in want of many things, are unhappy;
Therefore avaricious men are unhappy.

This example contains the substance of two syllogisms, which may be thus stated in regular form:

I.

Those who have many desires, are in want of many things;
Avaricious men have many desires;
Therefore avaricious men are in want of many things.

---

* Σωρὸς, *congeries, acervus.*

II.

Those, who want many things, are unhappy;
Avaricious men want many things
Therefore avaricious men are unhappy.

189. Every sorites may be resolved into as many syllogisms as it contains middle terms; or as it has propositions intervening between the first and the last. The second proposition of the sorites forms the major premise of the first syllogism; the third, the major of the second, and so on: The following example may be reduced to four syllogisms.

The mind is a thinking substance;
A thinking substance is a spirit;
A spirit has no composition of parts;
That, which has no composition of parts, is indissoluble;
That, which is indissoluble, is immortal;
Therefore the mind is immortal.

190. A sorites may be formed of hypothetical enthymemes, any number of which may be so joined in a series, that the consequent of each shall become the antecedent of the next following; in which case, by establishing the antecedent of the first we establish the consequent of the last; or, by removing the consequent of the last, we remove the antecedent of

the first. This is manifest in the following example:

If men are to be punished in another world, God must be the punisher;
If God be the punisher, the punishment must be just;
If the punishment be just, the punished must be guilty;
If the punished be guilty, they could have done otherwise;
If they could have done otherwise, they were free agents;
Therefore, if men are liable to punishment in another world, they must be free.*

CHAPTER EIGHTEENTH.

SOPHISMS.

191. A knowledge of the different kinds of reasoning, with their respective laws and principles, is of important use in enabling us to detect the sophistry and false reasoning employed in the support of error. But the rules of logick are of little service, till habit has rendered them familiar. By frequently examining the judgments and conclusions, which we have formed, and comparing them with those rules of procedure, which lead to certain results, we insensibly acquire the habit

* Common systems of Logick. Locke, Essay on the Understanding, p. iv. ch. 17.

of conducting our intellectual processes with accuracy, and also a facility in detecting the false deductions of others.

192. *Arguments, which contain a latent fallacy under the general appearance of correctness, are denominated sophisms.* They have been distinguished into various kinds, from which the following are selected, as those which are practised with the greatest frequency and success.

193. First. *Ignoratio Elenchi, a misapprehension of the question.* This sophism is committed when the arguments employed are of a nature to establish some other point, foreign to the question in debate; as if a person should attempt to prove, that Alfred the Great was a scholar, by affirming only, that he founded the University of Oxford; or, that Peter the Hermit was not a Christian, by proving that he was an ignorant fanatick. Neither of these facts has any necessary connexion with the question to be proved; for a man may be a patron of science, without being learned himself; and an ignorant fanatick may be a believer in Christianity.

194. Disputants are frequently guilty of this

fallacy, when, in the heat of controversy, they wander insensibly from the precise subject of discussion. It is also sometimes committed by design; as when a disputant, finding his adversary too powerful, or his position untenable, endeavours to gain an advantage by altering the question. The only effectual security against this species of sophistry is, to have the subject accurately defined, and to keep it steadily in view.

195. Secondly. *Petitio Principii, a begging of the question.* This consists in offering, as proof of a proposition, the substance of that proposition in other words. Thus a person attempts to prove, that God is eternal, by asserting that his existence is without beginning and without end. The proof and the question to be proved are substantially the same. This fallacy is often practised in familiar conversation. Thus a person asks, why opium induces sleep? He is answered, because it possesses a soporifick quality; which is equivalent to saying, that it induces sleep because it induces sleep. So we are told, that the grass grows by means of its vegetative power; and

that bodies tend to the centre, by reason of their gravitation.

196. Thirdly. *Arguing in a circle*. This is a kind of sophistry nearly related to the preceding; and consists in making two propositions reciprocally prove each other. Thus, the Papists prove the truth of the Scriptures, by the infallible testimony of the church; and then establish the infallibility of the church, by the authority of the Scriptures. The Necessarians practise this sophistry, when they bring their hypothesis to prove a fact, and then allege the fact, as proof of their hypothesis. They first assume, *gratuitously*, that the mind acts mechanically, like the body; and that it never can act, unless the motive, which causes the action, be greater than any other, then existing in the mind. Any particular volition is then declared to be *necessary*, because the motive which produced it, was the strongest then in the mind. But when asked for the proof, that this motive was the strongest, they simply refer us to the volition, which *otherwise* could not have taken place. That is, the *volition* was *necessary*, because it was produced by the *strongest motive ;* and the *motive* must

have been the *strongest*, because the *volition was produced*.

197. Fourthly. *Non causa pro causa;* or the assignation of a false cause. From an unwillingness to be thought ignorant, people often impose on themselves, and on the credulity of their fellow men, by assigning, as the cause of an event, something, that has no perceivable connexion with it. Among illiterate people, rare occurrences are sometimes thought to have a connexion, barely on account of their proximity in time or place. Thus, should the appearance of a comet be followed by a famine, pestilence, or any other grievous calamity, many people would consider the comet as the cause of that calamity. So, if a person have committed any flagrant crime, and shortly after meet with some distressing evil, the former is readily believed to have been the cause of the latter. This sophism is practised by all those impostors, who make pretensions to supernatural skill in interpreting enigmatical circumstances, and in presaging future events, from dreams and other omens; by which means they flatter the superstition and credulity of mankind.

198. Fifthly. Another species of sophistry is called *fallacia accidentis*. This consists in pronouncing concerning the general nature or properties of a thing, from some accidental circumstances. As when certain amusements are condemned, as universally unlawful, because they are occasionally carried to excess. So religion has been denounced, as an evil to mankind, because it has sometimes been assumed as a cover for crimes. If a medicine have operated unfavourably, weak persons are ready to reject it universally; or, if its good effects have been extraordinary, they are ready to adopt it in all cases whatsoever. This is the great cause of error, the substitution of local, partial, temporary connexions, for universal and unchangeable. The great remedy of error is the extensive observation and comparison of particulars, or laborious induction: and this is the true logick.

CHAPTER FIFTEENTH.

DISPOSITION OR METHOD.

199. Method, in logick, is a proper classification and arrangement of our thoughts on any

subject, either to facilitate the discovery of new truths, or to assist us in communicating to others truths already known; or, lastly, to enable us to preserve for future use the knowledge, which we have acquired. The disposition best adapted to the investigation of truth is the *analytick method;* which is therefore denominated the method of *invention;* and that which is best suited to the communication of knowledge, is the *synthetick method,* which for this reason has been called the method of *instruction.* In both of these methods, ideas are arranged in such order, as to exhibit their mutual connexions and relations.

200. *Analysis* *signifies an operation, by which some process of art is retraced, or some compound subject is reduced to its elementary parts. Synthesis† implies the act of collecting or putting together.* By the first we begin with the whole, and proceed by successive steps to the parts, of which it is composed: by the last we begin with the parts, or the most general principles, and proceed by combining them in due order to make up the whole.

---

* 'Αναλύω, *resolvo.*   † Συντίθημι, *conjungo, compone.*

201. *Analysis* and *synthesis* are terms of frequent use in many sciences, but they have not invariably the same signification annexed to them. They always, however, denote opposite processes, one beginning where the other terminates; and they reciprocally explain each other. They may be sometimes both employed with equal advantage in explaining the same thing. Thus, the mechanism of a complicated machine may be shown by either method. We may do it analytically, by taking the machine, in its entire state, and separating its parts in the reverse order of their combination, carefully explaining each part as we proceed, till we arrive at that, with which the mechanical construction commenced. Or we may adopt the synthetick method, and, beginning with the parts, in a state of separation, place them successively in their former order, till the combination is restored.

202. Most of the improvements in the different sciences and arts have been made by analysis. It is by this method, that things have been ranked into classes. A species is formed by analyzing individuals; and a genus by analyzing species. We practise the same meth

od in learning to read the language of our country. We first acquaint ourselves with the letters of the alphabet. We next trace out their powers, by observing in what manner they are sounded, as they are variously combined in syllables and words. In this way we at length acquire some general rules, by which we can readily give to each letter its appropriate sound, in any new combination. By the same method we learn a foreign language, and universal grammar; also the philosophy of mind, anatomy, chemistry, botany, and other branches of natural knowledge.

203. The synthetick method is not adapted to the investigation of new truths, and is rarely employed for that purpose. It is a process of composition; and consists in putting together a number of things in a particular manner, so as to accomplish some end proposed. But in order to do this, it is necessary for a person previously to possess the knowledge, which it is the object of the operation to evince. Without this knowledge, he would have nothing to guide him in the selection or arrangement of the parts; and would be in the condition of a man, who should undertake to make some very com

pound medicine, without knowing the ingredients of which it is composed. By successively mixing substances of different kinds, and in various proportions, directed only by casual circumstances or mere conjecture, it is possible for him ultimately to succeed; but this would not be likely to happen, till after much waste of time and many unsuccessful efforts.

204. The superiority of the analytick over the synthetick method, in the investigation of new truths, is very forcibly shown by Mr. Stewart in the following example: " Suppose
" a *knot*, of a very artificial construction, to be
" put into my hands, as an exercise for my
" ingenuity; and that I was required to inves-
" tigate a rule, which others, as well as myself,
" might be able to follow in practice, for mak-
"ing knots of the same sort. If I were to
" proceed in this attempt according to the
" spirit of a geometrical *synthesis*, I should
" have to try, one after another, all the vari-
" ous experiments, which my fancy could de-
" vise, till I had at last hit upon the particular
" knot I was anxious to tie. Such a process,
" however, would evidently be so completely

"tentative, and its final sucess would after all "be so extremely doubtful, that common sense "could not fail to suggest immediately the idea "of tracing the knot through all the various "complications of its progress, by cautiously "*undoing* or *unknitting* each successive turn "of the thread, in a retrograde order, from the "last to the first. After gaining this first step, "were all the former complications restored "again, by an inverse repetition of the same "operations, which I had performed in *undoing* "them, an infallible rule would be obtained for "solving the problem originally proposed."*

205. Though knowledge is chiefly acquired by the analytick method, it is most conveniently conveyed to others by the synthetick. The teacher uses one method, while the pupil practises the other. The synthetick method is the most plain, concise, and regular. It coincides with the order, in which the useful arts are practised, and most of the business of life is transacted. It begins with the most general and obvious principles, and leads the mind directly from known truths to those which are unknown. Instruction in every

* Elem. of the Phil. of the Mind, vol. ii. ch. 4, sect. 3.

science is given synthetically. It consists in prescribing rules more or less general; and these rules are nothing more than the results of analytical processes previously performed.

206. The other purpose of method is to secure to the mind a command over the knowledge it has acquired. Memory includes the power of treasuring up and preserving ideas; and also that of recalling them, when we have occasions for applying them to use. The latter power is usually termed *recollection*. In respect of both these faculties, the burden of memory is diminished by arranging the subjects of our knowledge under distinct heads, and charging the memory with some leading objects, only, in each class. But the same form of arrangement will not equally contribute to render the memory *retentive* and *ready*.* For this reason, no plan can be prescribed, which will be equally beneficial to all.

207. People, engaged in the active business of life, are under the necessity of carrying in their minds a multitude of particulars, which are of no further use, than to assist them in the daily business of their calling. To such per-

* Stewart, Elem. vol. 1. ch. 6, sect. 2.

sons a prompt recollection is of the highest importance, as it contributes to the despatch of business. They will therefore seek an arrangement, with reference to this object; and the surest method of effecting it is an arbitrary one, suggested by the circumstances of their situation, all which are of a local and temporary nature. While they continue their habitual pursuits, their thoughts will be successively called up by the objects offered to their senses: but on changing their situation, so as to lose their familiarity with those objects, the ideas, which were associated with them, must in a short time be irretrievably lost.

208. A different method of arrangement is necessary, to give the mind a durable possession of the acquisitions it has made. The only arrangement, capable of effecting this purpose, is that, which refers the truths, we are solicitous to preserve, to the general principles, with which they are connected. By having our ideas distributed according to this method, reason can lend its aid to the powers of memory, by tracing the natural relations and connexions of things, and thus deducing one truth from another. Some sort of arrangement or

other is indispensable to persons of every condition; otherwise but a small proportion of the thoughts, which pass through the mind, could by any effort be recalled.

CHAPTER SIXTEENTH.

RULES OF CONTROVERSY.

209. From the limited extent of human knowledge, and the different points of view, in which the same subjects may be contemplated by different minds, it follows of necessity, that a diversity of opinions must be entertained on many subjects of speculation. In whatever manner people are first led to form their opinions, they are usually disposed to defend them afterwards with zeal and pertinacity. Hence arise controversies and disputes, which are oftentimes conducted with such intemperate and misguided zeal, as to inflame animosities, by which the comfort and harmony of society are impaired.

210. These are the worst fruits of controversy. They are, however, merely incidental effects; and are counterbalanced by others of an opposite character, and of high inportance

to the interests of truth and virtue. The advantages of controversy consist in having questions of difficulty and moment settled in a satisfactory manner. The principles of government and law have been immovably fixed by the debates, which have passed in deliberative assemblies and in courts of justice.

211. All questions, not susceptible of rigorous demonstration, can be correctly settled only by a full and impartial comparison of the reasons on both sides. This is seldom done, with sufficient exactness, by the solitary investigation of an individual. Men rarely enter on the examination of a question wholly free from the bias of a previous opinion respecting it, which makes them more solicitous to find arguments for one side than for the other. It is only when the talents of different persons are enlisted, and opposite opinions are contended for, that questions are traced in all their bearings, and the grounds of an equitable decision are fully exhibited.

212. The importance of controversy may be inferred from the use, which has been made of it, in every period of the world. It has been adopted, as the principal mode of transacting

business, in the halls of legislation and in courts of justice, where questions of the deepest concern to individuals and communities are decided. The minds of youth have been trained to it in seminaries of education, where the practice of disputation, in various forms, has been preserved, as a salutary discipline of the mental powers.

213. As controversy, especially when carried on from motives of victory or reputation, is liable to be productive of evil rather than of good, it is incumbent on all, who engage in it, from whatever motives, to observe rigorously those laws and principles, by which the former may be avoided and the latter secured. The following rules, sometimes called canons of controversy, have been highly approved by writers of learning and discernment.*

214. Rule 1st. *The terms, in which the question in debate is expressed, and the precise point at issue, should be so clearly defined, that there could be no misunderstanding respecting them.* If this be not done, the dispute is liable to be, in a great degree, verbal. Arguments

---

* These rules are taken, with slight alterations, from the lectures of Dr. Hey, Norrisian Professor in the University of Cambridge. They may also be found in Kirwan's Logick, vol. ii.

will be misapplied, and the controversy protracted, because the parties engaged in it have different apprehensions of the question.

215. Rule 2d. *The parties should mutually consider each other, as standing on a footing of equality in respect to the subject in debate. Each should regard the other as possessing equal talents, knowledge, and desire for truth, with himself; and that it is possible, therefore, that he may be in the wrong, and his adversary in the right.* In the heat of controversy, men are apt to forget the numberless sources of error, which exist in every controverted subject, especially of *theology* and *metaphysicks*. Hence arise presumption, confidence, and arrogant language; all which obstruct the discovery of truth.

216. Rule 3d. *All expressions, which are unmeaning, or without effect in regard to the subject in debate, should be strictly avoided.* All expressions may be considered as unmeaning, which contribute nothing to the proof of the question; such as desultory remarks and declamatory expressions. To these may be added all technical, ambiguous, and equivocal expressions. These have a tendency to dazzle

and bewilder the mind, and to hinder its clear perception of the truth.

217. Rule 4th. *Personal reflections on an adversary should in no instance be indulged.* Whatever be his private character, his foibles are not to be named nor alluded to in a controversy. Personal reflections are not only destitute of effect, in respect to the question in discussion, but they are productive of real evil. They obstruct mental improvement, and are prejudicial to publick morals. They indicate in him, who uses them, a mind hostile to the truth; for they prevent even solid arguments from receiving the attention, to which they are justly entitled.

218. Rule 5th. *No one has a right to accuse his adversary of indirect motives.* Arguments are to be answered, whether he, who offers them, be sincere or not, especially as his want of sincerity, if real, could not be ascertained. To inquire into his motives, then, is useless. To ascribe indirect ones to him is worse than useless; it is hurtful.

219. Rule 6th. *The consequences of any doctrine are not to be charged on him, who maintains it, unless he expressly avows them.* If an absurd

consequence be fairly deducible from any doctrine, it is rightly concluded that the doctrine itself is false; but it is not rightly concluded, that he, who advances it, supports the absurd consequence. The charitable presumption, in such case, would be, that he had never made the deduction; and that, if he had made it, he would have abandoned the original doctrine.

220. Rule 7th. *As truth, and not victory, is the professed object of controversy, whatever proofs may be advanced, on either side, should be examined with fairness and candour; and any attempt to ensnare an adversary by the arts of sophistry, or to lessen the force of his reasoning, by wit, cavilling, or ridicule, is a violation of the rules of honourable controversy.*

CHAPTER SEVENTEENTH.

RULES OF INTERPRETATION.

221. To ascertain the true meaning of a written document is often difficult and embarrassing, even when it is of recent date and in our own language; but the difficulty is greatly enhanced, when the writing is in a foreign language, or has descended from ancient times

RULES OF INTERPRETATION. 163

222. The circumstances, which aggravate the labour of the interpreter, are numerous, and of various kinds. No branch of knowledge is entirely exempt from them; but they exist in the greatest degree in those sciences, which involve our most important interests, both sacred and civil. For this reason, principles and rules of interpretation have been carefully formed for developing the true meaning of the sacred Scriptures and of legal instruments.

223. The design of interpretation is to ascertain the real intention of the writer; to develope the true meaning of his words, where they are obscure or ambiguous; and to determine what was his design, where his words do it but imperfectly. The following rules are of a general character, and may be employed with equal advantage, in explaining writings of every kind:

224. Rule 1st. The interpreter of a written document must have a thorough knowledge of the language, in which it is written.

225. Rule 2d. He must possess an intimate acquaintance with the subject of the writing. Many words have different significations in different sciences and arts; and the particular

meaning they were intended to convey, in any instance, must be agreeable to the nature of the subject, on which they were employed.

226. Rule 3d. The true interpretation of a writing often requires a knowledge of the character of its author. His peculiar bent of mind, his temperament, his vocation, and especially his political or religious tenets, may have had an influence, for which some allowance should be made.

227. Rule 4th. If the writing to be interpreted be of ancient date, the interpreter should ascertain the genuineness of his text; whether it has descended to him as it came from the author, without any corruptions or interpolations from other hands.

228. Rule 5th. The interpreter should also be well acquainted with the history of the country and of the period, in which his author wrote. Words have different meanings in different ages; and writers are insensibly influenced by the existing fashions, and other circumstances of a local and temporary nature.

229. Rule 6th. The mind of the interpreter should be wholly free from all antecedent bias in favour of any system, doctrine, or creed.

which might influence his judgment, in the interpretation he is about to make.

230. Rule 7th. In making the interpretation of a document, the subject and predicate of each proposition should be carefully distinguished; the various sentences and clauses should be construed in reference to each other; and the resulting sense of all the parts should be connected and consistent.

231. Rule 8th. Words, which admit of different senses, should be taken in their most common and obvious meaning, unless such a construction lead to absurd consequences, or be inconsistent with the known intention of the writer.

232. Rule 9th. When any word or expression is ambiguous, and may, consistently with common use, be taken in different senses, it must be taken in that sense, which is agreeable to the subject, of which the writer was treating.

233. Rule 10th. Doubtful words and phrases must always be construed in such a sense as will make them produce some effect; and not in such a sense as will render them wholly nugatory,

234. Rule 11th. Violations of the rules of grammar do not vitiate a writing, in which the sense is distinctly expressed. When a passage is imperfect, or unintelligible, the interpreter is at liberty to supply such words, as are manifestly necessary to render its sense complete. But he is not allowed, in a similar case, to expunge certain words from the text, in order to give an intelligible meaning to those that remain.

235. Rule 12th. When there are no special reasons for the contrary, words should be construed in their literal, rather than in their figurative sense; relative words should be referred to the nearest, rather than to a remote antecedent; and words, which are capable of being understood in either, should be taken in their generick, rather than in their specifick sense.

236. Rule 13th. However general may be the words, in which a covenant is expressed, it comprehends those things, only, on which it appears the parties intended to contract, and not those, which they had not in view. But when the object of the covenant is an universality of things, it comprehends all the particu

lar things, which compose that universality, even those, of which the parties had no knowledge.

237. Rule 14th. Whatever is obscure or doubtful in a covenant should be interpreted by the intention of the parties. If the intention of the parties does not appear from the words of the covenant, it should be inferred from the existing customs and usages of the place, in which it was made. If the words of a covenant contradict the well known intention of the parties, this intention must be regarded rather than the words.*

238. Rule 15th. When former interpreters are appealed to, in order to establish the sense of an ancient writing, those, *cæteris paribus*, should be preferred, who were nearest the author, in time or place, as his children, pupils, correspondents, or countrymen; and who had, therefore, better advantages for knowing his mind, than more distant commentators.

* Satri, Dialect. Instit. Kirwan, Logick. Le Clerc, Ars Critica. Vattel, Law of Nations. Rutherforth, Lectures on Grotius. Gilbert, Law of Evidence. Pothier on Obligations. Domat on the Civil Law.

CONCLUDING REMARKS.

In the preceding summary, an attempt has been made to state and explain those rules of intellectual discipline, which may guide and improve the reasoning faculties. As the work is intended to be strictly elementary, general principles only have been given, with such plain examples, as might limit and illustrate their meaning. The following remarks are subjoined for the use of those, who may wish to extend their inquiries on the subject of logick, and the philosophy of the human mind.

Dr. Reid's analysis of Aristotle's Logick contains a brief but comprehensive exposition of the syllogistick system. A more full account of the categories, together with the various laws of syllogistick reasoning, may be found in the logical treatises of Burgersdicius and of Le Clerc.

Of modern systems of logick, those of Watts and of Duncan have been most approved. A more recent and valuable treatise, than either of these, is that of Kirwan.

It is essential to accurate reasoning to distinguish those first principles of human knowl edge, which must be taken for granted, from those propositions, which require proof. On this subject the treatise of Father Buffier, entitled First Truths, Beattie's Essay on Truth, and Condillac on the Origin of Knowledge, are valuable sources of information.

The Novum Organum of Lord Bacon contains in a small compass those rules of inductive logick, which have been followed with the happiest success, both in physical researches, and in the philosophy of the mind.

On the subject of moral reasoning, important information may be derived from Gambier's Introduction to Moral Evidence, and from the first book of Campbell's Philosophy of Rhetorick.

For the general direction of the mind, in its researches after truth, rules of a more practical nature may be found in Locke's Conduct of the Understanding, and Watts on the Improvement of the Mind.

The study of those authors, who reason clearly and accurately, is one of the best methods of improving the reasoning powers. For this purpose, Berkeley on the Principles of Human Knowledge, Wollaston on the Religion of Nature, and Baxter on the Soul, may be read with great advantage. The catalogue might easily be extended if it were thought necessary. It will be concluded by referring the student to the metaphysical writings of Locke, Reid, Stewart, and Brown. They may be consulted with great benefit, on each of the subjects above mentioned; and may be said to comprise in themselves a complete system of intellectual philosophy.

But the student should remember, that neither learning the best rules, nor reading the best models, can supersede the necessity of intent and continued reflection. He should dwell on the operations of his own mind, and mark the difficulties, which prevent his arriving at clear conclusions; whether they arise from misapprehension of the subject, from the ambiguity of language, from weakness in the power of attention, or from the biases of association. He will thus insensibly form a logick for himself, which, while it embraces the rules, common to all minds, will be peculiarly adapted to the improvement of his own.

NOTES AND ILLUSTRATIONS.

Note A, page 17.

I HAVE used *reflection* and *consciousness* as synonymous terms, and they are so used by eminent writers on pneumatology. Some, however, have considered them as denoting operations specifically different. Dr. Reid says, " reflection ought to be distinguished from consciousness, with which it is too often confounded, even by Mr. Locke. All men are conscious of the operations of their own minds, at all times while they are awake, but there are few who reflect on them, or make them the objects of their thought. Though the mind is conscious of its operations, it does not attend to them; its attention is turned solely to the external objects, about which those operations are employed."* In another place he says, that " attention to things external is properly called *observation*, and attention to the subjects of our consciousness, *reflection*." This definition of *reflection* is substantially the same with that of Mr. Locke, which I have used.

The foregoing passage from Dr. Reid points out a difference in degree, rather than in kind, between consciousness and reflection. It is true that the bulk of mankind

* Intellectual Powers, Essay 1.

pay very little attention to their mental operations. But, without some degree of attention, they would have no consciousness of them whatever; and so far as they do attend to them, so far, according to Dr. Reid's own account, they reflect.

The only way, by which the phenomena of the mind can be investigated, is by attending to its successive changes and operations, as they are passing; and this reflex act of attention is nothing more than an effort of the mind to increase or prolong the consciousness of its own acts. Reflection on any operation of the mind presupposes the actual existence of that operation. It may be examined afterwards by the assistance of memory, but this subsequent examination cannot be denominated reflection, agreeably to the strict sense of that word. Are we then to believe, that reflection and consciousness are two distinct simultaneous efforts; and each of them different from the operation, which the mind is carrying on at the same time? This would oblige us to consider the mind, not as simple, but as a complication of different powers or agents, one of which may be employed in watching the operations of another, while its own acts are examined by a third.

Dr. Reid defines reflection, "*attention to the subjects of our consciousness.*" By this expression he evidently supposes consciousness and the subjects of consciousness to be different things. But the mind can be conscious only of what passes within itself. Consciousness, then, according to him, means the notice, which the mind takes of its own operations. Now, as he places reflection in attention to the subjects of our consciousness, and it appears manifest, that by the subjects of consciousness he means nothing else than the operations of the mind, it follows, even from his own statement, that these terms are but different names for the same thing.

In common use there seems to be a slight difference in the import of these terms. By consciousness is commonly understood barely the mind's notice or perception of its own acts and modes of existence. But reflection is usually employed to express some degree of voluntary attention to the phenomena of the mind, in order to ascertain the laws, by which it is governed. As the bulk of mankind have no curiosity for such speculations, they have been said rarely, if ever, to reflect.

Note B, page 121.

Logicians have, from the earliest period, denominated the predicate of the conclusion the *major term*, and its subject, the *minor*. The only reason, assigned for doing this, is, that the predicate of a proposition has a wider extension than the subject. But this is not a sufficient reason for calling it the major term, since, in all our affirmations and negations, we are invariably governed by the comprehension of terms, without the slightest regard to their extension. We assert the more general of he less general, for this manifest reason, that the former is a part of the latter. We predicate the genus of the pecies, but not the species of the genus. The predicate of a proposition is only an attribute of the subject; and in this light it must be viewed, in order to render the proposition true. When, for example, we affirm that saffron is yellow, we refer a single property to a subject, in which it is known to coexist with several other properties. In doing this, we are guided by our knowledge of that plant without inquiring what other bodies there are in existence, which have a yellow colour. And we proceed in the same way, when the predicate has no greater extension than the subject, as when we affirm that iron is susceptible of magnetical attraction.

In passing from one rank of beings to another, in the order of their classification, we observe that each superior class stands in the next below it. Thus we may say a mastiff is a dog, a dog is an animal, and an animal is a being, that has life, sense, &c. It is obvious that the first subject contains each of the predicates that follow.

As, in an act of judgment, one thing is perceived to be contained in another, so, in syllogistick reasoning, one proposition is shown to be contained in another, that in a third, and so on. This process has been aptly illustrated by a collection of boxes of different sizes, placed one in another. In such a nest of boxes, it would be natural to say of that which was placed first, and contained all the rest, that it was the largest box, and of that, which was in the centre, and had no other in it, that it was the least box. But, in giving names to the three terms of a syllogism, this rule of common sense has been violated. The less is made to contain the greater. The predicate of the conclusion, which is contained in each of the other two, is called the major term, and the sub ject of the conclusion, which contains both the others, is called the minor term.

Note C, page 122.

This is true in that arrangement of parts, which renders the syllogism the most simple and the most perfect; though it will not hold in all those technical forms, in which it has been expressed.

It may not be deemed wholly impertinent in this place to give a brief description of that celebrated doctrine of modes and figures, in which simple syllogisms are involved, in the ancient books of logick. By the *mode* of a syllogism is meant the designation of the quantity and quality of its propositions. By *figure* is meant the situation of the middle term with respect to the major and minor terms. As the middle term occurs in each of the premises, it is susceptible of four different positions in relation to the extremes. Hence four figures have been invented. In the first, the middle term is the subject of the major proposition, and the predicate of the minor. In the second, it is the predicate, and in the third, the subject, of both the premises. In the fourth, it is the predicate of the major premise, and the subject of the minor.

Each of the four figures has several modes, which are designated by the vowels, A, E, I, O; characters, employed by logicians to denote the quantity and quality of propositions. A, placed before a proposition, denotes that it is an universal affirmative ; E denotes an universal negative ; I, a particular affirmative ; and O, a particular negative. To assist the memory, the following couplet was contrived :

Asserit, A, negat E, verùm generalitèr ambæ.
Asserit I, negat O, sed particularitèr ambo.

As all the possible combinations of three of these four letters, in three propositions, amount to sixty-four, this number of modes might be formed. But, of these, fifty-three are excluded by certain established rules, and one rejected, as useless ; leaving only ten, that are considered as legitimate. Several of these are repeated in different figures, so as to make, in the whole, nineteen conclusive modes. Each mode is furnished with an appropriate name, consisting of three syllables, and containing three of the vowels before named. The three syllables of the mode are placed before the propositions of the syllogism, in order that the vowel letter, which alone is regarded, may indicate the quantity and quality of the proposition, before which it stands.

To the first figure are given four modes; which are denominated Barbara, Celarent, Darii, Ferio. The second figure has likewise four modes, namely, Cæsare, Camestres, Festino, Baroco. The third has six modes, Darapti, Felapton, Disamis, Datisi, Bocardo, Ferison. The fourth has five modes, Bamarip, Camenes, Dimatis, Festapo, Fression.

These barbarous words have been thus formed into hexameter verses;

Barbara, Celarent, Darii, Ferio quoque, primæ.
Cæsare, Camestres, Festino, Baroco, secundæ.
Tertia Darapti sibi vindicat atque Felapton;
Adjungens Disamis, Datisi, Bocardo, Ferison.
Non Bamarip, Camenes, Dimatis, Festapo, Fresison.

EXAMPLES.

Figure First.

Bar- Every animal has sensation;
Ba- Every man is an animal;
Ra. Therefore every man has sensation.

Ce- No opinions, hurtful to the morals of society, should be embraced;
La- Atheistical sentiments are hurtful to the morals of society;
Rent. Therefore atheistical sentiments should not be embraced.

Da- All good men love peace;
Ri- Some statesmen are good men;
I. Therefore some statesmen love peace.

Fe- No man of dissolute habits is a safe companion;
Ri- Some men of learning are dissolute in their habits;
O. Therefore some men of learning are not safe companions.

Figure Second.

Ca- Every virtuous man is fit to be believed;
Mes- No liar is fit to be believed;
Tres. Therefore no liar is a virtuous man.

Ba- Every true patriot tries to promote the publick good;
Ro- Some men in high stations do not try to promote the publick good;
Co. Therefore some men in high stations are not true patriots.

Figure Third.

Da- All good Christians will be saved;
Rap- All good Christians have sinned;
Ti. Therefore some, who have sinned, will be saved

Examples of the other modes may readily be formed.

FINIS.

www.ingramcontent.com/pod-product-compliance
Lightning Source LLC
Chambersburg PA
CBHW071426160426
43195CB00013B/1828